I0796674

Argentine Skyhawks in the Falklands War

Argentine Skyhawks in the Falklands War

Targeting the Task Force in the South Atlantic in 1982

Salvador Mafé Huertas

With Santiago Rivas

First published in Great Britain in 2025 by
Air World
An imprint of Pen & Sword Books Limited
Yorkshire – Philadelphia

ISBN 978 1 03612 688 9

A CIP catalogue record for this book is available from the British Library.

Typeset by Mac Style
Printed in the UK by CPI Group (UK) Ltd, Croydon, CR0 4YY.

The Publisher's authorised representative in the EU for product safety is Authorised Rep Compliance Ltd., Ground Floor, 71 Lower Baggot Street, Dublin D02 P593, Ireland.
www.arccompliance.com

For a complete list of Pen & Sword titles please contact

PEN & SWORD BOOKS LIMITED
47 Church Street, Barnsley, South Yorkshire, S70 2AS, England
E-mail: enquiries@pen-and-sword.co.uk
Website: www.pen-and-sword.co.uk
or
PEN AND SWORD BOOKS
1950 Lawrence Road, Havertown, PA 19083, USA
E-mail: uspen-and-sword@casematepublishers.com
Website: www.penandswordbooks.com

To my friend Jorge Portales Alberola, an excellent photographer

Contents

Introduction

This book is intended for those with an interest in military aviation, and especially naval air operations on aircraft carriers.

In this account, as objective as possible, I have tried to avoid value judgements, which will be left to the reader, and my greatest commitment was to try to cover the different levels of specific knowledge on the subject of those who read it.

I apologize to those familiar with the subject for simplifying the terminology to make it easier to follow for those who are not used to it. That is why terms such as altitude, altitude and flight level, or indicated, true or absolute speed, are unified in order not to complicate the core of the story.

The Argentine Navy had the Skyhawk in their ranks, being the first jet to be catapulted from a Latin American aircraft carrier and, although overshadowed by the actions of the Super Étendard, one of its main achievements in the Falklands War was the sinking of the frigate HMS *Ardent*.

The old A-4B and C of the Argentine Air Force have been giving way, since 1997, to the new McDonnell Douglas A-4AR and OA-4AR Fightinghawk, modernized versions of the A-4M, which are currently the only combat jets of that force, although from 2025 it will start to receive the first of twenty-four F-16AM/BM Vipers acquired from Denmark.

In this way, including the aircraft that were not finally delivered and those that were delivered to use as spare parts, Argentina purchased a total of 165 A-4 Skyhawks (129 for the Air Force and 36 for the Navy).

Acknowledgements

This work would have been not possible without the help provided by former Tercera Escuadrilla Aeronaval de Caza y Ataque pilots Castro Fox, Philippi, Arca and Lecour, the Comando de Aviación Naval, the Naval Attaché at the Argentine Embassy in Madrid, Grupo 5 de Caza pilots Cervera, Sánchez and Carballo plus Dave Morgan, Rafael Treviño Martínez and Santiago Rivas.

Chapter 1

Replacing the First Generation Carrier Jet

In 1963, due to the obsolescence of its fighter/attack force, Naval Aviation made the decision to replace the Vought F4U-5 Corsair and Grumman F9F-2 Panther, which generated a series of studies and it was concluded that the aircraft indicated for replacing the Corsair was the Douglas AD-5 Skyraider and to replace the Panther, the Douglas A-4 Skyhawk. In mid-1966 the Armada was interested in acquiring the A-4B, although the United States counter-offered a batch of thirty A-4As that was not considered. In 1968, the necessary steps were taken to buy ten A-4F and two TA-4F aircraft and, once again, the agreement of the Americans was not obtained. For that reason in 1969, Britain was asked for a quote for twelve Hawker Siddeley Harrier GR.Mk 1 aircraft. Having obtained these and taking advantage of the trip to Argentina of the recently-acquired ARA (Armada República Argentina) *25 de Mayo* (V-2) aircraft carrier, tests were carried out on its flight deck on 4 September 1969. In this situation and to prevent the purchase of the British jets, the United States offered the A-4B Skyhawk, reaching an agreement.

Naval Aviation decided that their aircraft should have different equipment than the A-4Bs that the Fuerza Aérea Argentina (FAA – Argentine Air Force) had had since 1966. It was decided that they would be equipped with TACAN, ADF, VOR/ILS, UHF/VHF (somewhat different from the FAA A-4Bs which had not retained TACAN and UHF). To this end, a commission travelled to Villa Reynolds, where everything related to it was studied and it was decided that the wings would be equipped with Spoilers, in addition to an engine with more thrust (the one corresponding to the A-4C was adopted).

Taking advantage of the fact that the BAe HS-125 Dominie acquired for the force was being brought to the country, Rear Admiral Hermes Quijada visited Israel to exchange opinions and information, since the Israeli A-4E pilots had obtained invaluable experience in the Yom Kippur war. They suggested that a purchase of A-4Bs be made to upgrade to the A-4Q level and some A-4Bs, and at a lower cost, to be used for training. Finally, due to restrictions from the United States, sixteen A-4Qs and eight A-4Bs were purchased, although the latter were used as spare parts, all for a total of $5 million.

On 1 May 1971, the contract was signed and a commission was formed that would initially train in this type of aircraft in the V Air Brigade, while Ensign (TF) Julio Lavezzo was designated to carry out test flights in the A-4 and the Replacement Air Group in the US Navy VT-21 Squadron. Meanwhile, the squadron members travelled to Villa Reynolds and then went on to operate in another US Navy squadron, VA-127, where they conducted training on A-4s aboard the aircraft carrier USS *Coral Sea*.

During this stage a very curious anecdote happened in which Lieutenant Commander (CC) Invierno was the protagonist, when he was performing the daytime qualification in marginal weather conditions in the Pacific Ocean and far from the coast. In the last approach he had to enter Bingo (amount of fuel needed to reach the alternative on the ground) and with eight planes in circuit, Lieutenant Commander Invierno found the deck occupied by a plane from the US squadron (also in training) that had been delayed in the cables. As the weather was bad, he was singled out for the alternative (he did not know what it was because it had changed). Quickly the LSO (Ensign Lavezzo) changed the aircraft carrier's control frequency and learned that the ship had ceased operations, that Lieutenant Commander Winter was already on layer 8/8 (completely covered in clouds) and that a tanker plane had already stopped and gathered him. Then it was learned that he had landed on an island of which he never knew the name. He spent the night there and the next day, as the weather conditions improved and with the ship's deck cleared, he returned on board.

Part of the commission stationed in the United States returned to the country and Lieutenant Commander Invierno (commander) and Nabias and Lieutenants (TN) Saralegui and Troitino, travelled to Jacksonville, where they would carry out the test flights in the factory. The machines were in good condition and before delivery they flew an average of five hours per plane. A programme similar to that of the Argentine Air Force was made. AIM-9B Sidewinder missiles (twenty units) and the Sargent Flecher Buddy Pack in-flight refuelling tanks were also purchased, although as always there was one detail: Sidewinders had first been ordered along with refuelling tanks and were denied by the United States. For this reason, Israel was resorted to, offering the Shafrir 2 missile. As soon as that offer was obtained, the Americans counter-offered the AIM-9B Sidewinder which was much cheaper, but of lower performance than the Shafrir 2. The refuelling tanks could be purchased along with an order from Israel, but also could not be obtained.

The Buddy Pack has a capacity of 900 litres of fuel and, when refuelling to another aircraft, once consumed, automatically transfers the fuel from the wing tanks. The A-4Q consumed the fuel in the following order: first the auxiliary tanks, then the wings and finally the tank behind the cabin.

Once all the planes were in Jacksonville, on 7 February they boarded the carrier ARA *25 de Mayo* with all the spare parts and ammunition. The ship set sail on 10 February towards the Puerto Belgrano Naval Base (BNPB) and arrived on 3 March in the morning. The planes were directly incorporated into the Tercera Escuadrilla Aeronaval de Caza y Ataque. The original idea was to form a Flotilla made up of two Squadrons, one for Training (eight A-4B aircraft) and one Operational (sixteen A-4Q aircraft). Such an idea later could not be realized and only remained as the Third Naval Fighter and Attack Squadron belonging to Naval Wing No. 3.

Aircraft 3-A-209 had the honour of being the first Skyhawk to carry out an operational landing on board on 14 August 1972, under the command of Lieutenant Commander Invierno. Two days later, the first catapult launch was carried out. Weapons training was carried out in the Trelew and Isla Verde industrial estates.

A commission made up of technicians from the unit had to travel from 28 June to 14 July 1972 to Australia to board the aircraft carrier HMAS *Melbourne* to learn the experiences that this country had with the A-4G since the ship was similar to *25 de Mayo*. This was necessary since during the catapult phase the strobe recovery equipment (Type AA Mk 1) worked incorrectly, causing breakdowns in the aircraft, since it required a different regulation of its elements to operate with this type of aircraft.

The incorporation into active service of the A-4Q Skyhawk was a great technological advance. For the first time, the Embarked Naval Group had a modern and effective attack component, with equipment such as infrared air-to-air missiles and in-flight refuelling capability. In the rest of Latin America this capacity was only reached by Brazil in 1999.

On 16 January 1973, when Ensign Mario Peña, who had recently returned from the United States to carry out the adaptation in the A-4, was conducting a formation flight with Lieutenant Carlos Ruiz in the vicinity of the Base Aeronaval Comandante Espora (BACE), both started a loop, with Lieutenant Peña as numeral (flying 3-A-216). At the exit of the manoeuvre, the plane was out of control, after which he ejected correctly, although at that moment the hose of the oxygen mask caught on the throttle lever, which is why he choked and died instantly. After this unfortunate event, a report came from the United States regarding this danger, stating that the hose should be passed through an eyelet; the truth is that when NCO Dreiling did the investigation, when he found the pilot's helmet, since he found the mask holder fastened on the helmet without the mask, he deduced that it had to have been hooked on the throttle. Indeed, after the expert opinion, the appreciation of the NCO was certain. The uncontrolled manoeuvre that TF Peña suffered was a situation that was currently being investigated in the United States, where a very large study was carried out that reached Argentina after the fatal accident of Lieutenant Eduardo Marty (3-A-215) that occurred on 25 June 1973 in Monte Hermoso, Bahía Blanca, in the same way regarding the lack of control of the plane. Marty managed to eject, but was never recovered. What happened was that in a manoeuvre called 'departure' the tail lift would come out of the air flow losing its lift and then control of the plane. In both cases they were performing vertical manoeuvres (curls).

Previously, during the month of September 1972, the Skyhawks participated in their first exercise, which UNITAS XIII, together with the US Navy.

In 1973, when where transferred to the 3rd Naval Wing, the callsigns became 3-A-301 to 316.

On 30 April 1974, another accident occurred, when 3-A-305 commanded by Ensign Roberto Curilovic and 3-A-314 with Lieutenant Augusto Bedacarratz collided in flight, the leader losing the horizontal stabilizer and the second suffering damage to theirs, although both were able to land.

These accidents proved the need for pilots to receive training in two-seater aircraft and the purchase of two examples of the TA-4J was studied, in addition to receiving an offer from Lockheed to modify two aircraft in a similar way to the Singapore TA-4S, but neither could be carried out due to lack of funds, instead it being agreed with the US Navy to send pilots to the VT-21 and 22 Squadrons, equipped with the TA-4J.

The third fatal accident occurred on 13 June 1975 at 10:15 when Ensign Echegoyen, in 3-A-210, was performing a 'Bolter' on board the aircraft carrier. Due to the delay in the acceleration of the engine, which had a very low speed after the touchdown on deck, the plane plunged into the sea on the ship's port side. Unfortunately the pilot ejected too low and was killed.

Ensign Carlos Sánchez Alvarado suffered another accident when on 23 September 1975, at 17:35, when hooking with 3-A-313 on the cable No. 1, it broke and the aircraft fell into the sea. The pilot ejected and fell onto the deck of the ship, but the wind inflated his parachute and threw him into the water. Then he was recovered by an Alouette III helicopter (registration 3-H-9).

In 1974, the squadron was visited by an Israeli pilot who had flown the A-4E and exchanged experiences gained in the Six Day and Yom Kippur Wars. The years 1977 to 1979 were the glory days of the Third Squadron, when they normally operated from the aircraft carrier with up to eleven A-4Qs.

That year the possibility of buying twenty A-4Cs was studied, then reduced to eighteen, with deliveries in 1976. In addition, four additional A-4Cs and four TA-4Js would be purchased, with which four TA-4Cs would be made, using the rear and wings of the single seaters with the front of the two-seaters, thus leaving four aircraft. These should be delivered between July and August 1976. A similar proposal had been delivered to the Argentine Air Force and another to the Uruguayan Air Force, although the lack of budget ended by the cancellation of said operation, both for the COAN and the FAA.

In 1976 it was decided to put into service two of the received A-4Bs, which had received wings and nose modified to the A-4Q standard and some work began to put them into service, but they were suspended in 1978 and their parts were used to put more aircraft in service for the 1982 conflict.

However, the idea of obtaining more A-4s was maintained and in 1977 the purchase of a lot of A-4Fs was requested, but the United States did not authorize the acquisition, citing the lack of aircraft available for sale; later on the possibility of buying new A-4Ms was ruled out, finally leading to the purchase of the Dassault Super Étendard and the idea of incorporating the Harrier was returned to, this time thinking of the Sea Harrier FRS.Mk 1, with the aim of receiving them for 1984 to replace A-4Qs.

During 1977 and 1978 most of the pilots reached the Centurion qualification, which means that they had made more than 100 arrested landings (carrier traps). During the Seventh Sea Stage, the evaluation of night operation of the A-4Q was carried out on aircraft carriers, where all the pilots of the squadron were catapulted at night and only one arrested landing was carried out in the dark of the morning by Augusto Bedacarratz. Then the Fleet Commander suspended the evaluation and only operated day or twilight, this meant that it could be catapulted at night and thus have the ability to attack the enemy in the early light of dawn.

On 28 September 1977, while carrying out exercises with the aircraft carrier, the destroyer ARA *Comodoro Py* detected an unidentified aircraft off the coast of the province of Santa Cruz, ordering the launch of the A-4Qs to intercept it, although contact was lost before take-off.

Shortly thereafter, on 3 February 1978, five A-4Qs were deployed to the Almirante Zar Naval Air Base, in Trelew, as part of Operation Rigel, while a destroyer was deployed to the area to carry out radar detection of any possible intruder approaching the base, returning to Espora on the 13th.

To improve training, in March Lieutenant Commander Lavezzo launched the first of two AIM-9B Sidewinder missiles from 3-A-301. At that time, the purchase of AIM-9E or AIM-9J missiles was being studied, and equipping the aircraft with 30mm DEFA cannon, as the Air Force subsequently did.

The tense situation with Chile continued throughout the year, requiring the squadron to maintain a high degree of enlistment and training, reaching a total of seventeen pilots and eleven aircraft. At the end of 1978, the border conflict with Chile broke out in the Beagle Channel area. Given the seriousness of the situation, the squadron travelled to Mendoza and carried out four dissimilar air combat training missions with F-86F Sabre aircraft of the Argentine Air Force, these simulating the Chilean Hawker Hunter. Shortly thereafter, upon the detection of a Learjet 25 aircraft from the Chilean Air Force at the Almirante Zar Naval Base, in Trelew, Chubut province, Operation Rigel II was carried out between 31 August and 7 September, with the deployment of six A-4Qs to intercept potential intruders, with the destroyer ARA *Piedrabuena* as a radar picket.

In the face of the almost imminent conflict, the aircraft formations were prepared, with an attack configuration with four aircraft, of which two would carry on their supports three LAU-69 pods with nineteen 70mm rocket tubes and two with six Mk 82 bombs with Snakeye brake tails. They could also use the 127mm ZUNI Mk 24 rockets from LAU-10 four-tube launchers. The planes would be guided in the attack by either the S-2E Tracker from the aircraft carrier or the land-based Lockheed SP-2H Neptune. For night missions, an A-4Q was equipped with Mk 24 or Mk 45 flares. For its part, 3-A-309 was equipped with a chaff launcher and flares.

Ensign Petinari had to prepare the armament for the aircraft, for which the F4-U Corsair intervalometer bomb system was adapted for all the aircraft. This apparatus programmed the bombs dropping so that they are launched according to the chosen sequence.

On 8 December, the entire fleet was deployed to the south with the aircraft carrier as the flagship, and eleven A-4Qs embarked within the framework of Operation Thunderer. Once in the conflict zone, the squadron commander, Lieutenant Commander Ítalo Lavezzo, ordered reconnaissance and patrol flights, making two interceptions of Chilean planes that were tracking the fleet to the east of Tierra del Fuego. At all times there was an interceptor ready on deck to be catapulted, armed with two Sidewinder air-to-air missiles, with external tanks and with the pilot on board. The patrols were individual and there were two planes patrolling separately at the same time. The first interception was carried out by the squadron commander on 15 December at 14:40, at the controls of 3-A-301, along with Ensign Poch in 3-A-307, which were launched upon detection two targets on the radar. Upon finding the first of them, it turned out to be an own S-2A Tracker on a transport flight from Río Grande to Ushuaia, while later they intercepted a CASA C-212 Aviocar of the Chilean Navy that was tracking the fleet east of Tierra del

Fuego, flying at 5,000ft. Lavezzo activated the armament panel and selected the missiles, asking for instructions, but was instructed by the Fleet Commander, Admiral Barbuzi, not to fire, but to report the position and movements of the C-212. After passing near the Chilean plane, he began to return to the aircraft carrier, while the C-212 tried to fly as fast as possible towards the clouds to get out of sight. At no time was there radio contact.

Another interception was carried out by Ensign Petinari at 04:49 on 19 December, flying 3-A-301, of another C-212 aircraft, carrying out the same mission as the one before at 3,000ft.

In 1979, although the tension had decreased, the force maintained its presence in the south, deploying the A-4Qs to the Río Grande Naval Base in May, and from 28 April to 9 June they operated aboard the aircraft carrier. In the Third Sea Stage of the year, from 2 to 11 July, Type 275 napalm bombs purchased in Spain were evaluated, in addition to 250lb Mk 81 bombs and LACO 7 and 19-tube rocket launchers for 70mm EDESA Albatros rockets of domestic production. Also, during Operation Gaviota, on 5 November 1979, 70kg Condib Mk 70 anti-runway bombs were tested.

From 27 June to 11 July 1980 they participated for the first time in an exercise with the Brazilian Navy, the Fraterno, where they operated with the frigates *Defensora* and *Constitução*.

On 10 September of that year, planes 3-A-302, 305, 207 and 312 were deployed to Río Grande, in the face of a new increase in tension with Chile, leaving two on 30-minute alert for an attack with LAU rockets, one with Sidewinders and the other with LAU-69 rockets. On 12 September the corvette ARA *Guerrico* issued a red alert to a possible target and at 15:23 3-A-302 and 305 took off, although contact with it was lost and the planes returned. Later, as the tension decreased, the planes returned to their base.

In 1981 the last loss occurred before the Falklands War, 3-A-203, when on 9 August Lieutenant Castro Fox caught the No 4 cable, but it broke, the Skyhawk plunged into the sea and its pilot was rescued with serious injuries, by triggering the ejection already underwater. This aircraft was a veteran of US operations from USS *Essex* over the Bay of Pigs, Cuba, in 1961.

During that year activity was reduced, since several of the pilots were sent to France to train in the Super Étendard. In addition, fuel losses were detected in the planes, which left the fleet on the ground until the problem was corrected.

Lieutenant Ítalo Lavezzo after making his solo A-4Q flight in the United States in July 1971. This was the only A-4Q to receive the word 'Navy' on the front of the fuselage.

Transfer of the A-4Qs upon arrival, after being disembarked from the aircraft carrier, from the Puerto Belgrano Naval Base to the Comandante Espora Naval Air Station.

A-4Q 0658/A-205 with two 300-gallon tanks and a Sargent Fletcher refuelling tank in the centre pylon. This plane was lost in an accident in 1986. In the photo it can be seen with the unit's crest below the cockpit.

0657/A-204 in low-speed flight. Currently this aircraft is preserved as a gate guard at the building of the General Staff of the Argentine Navy, in Buenos Aires.

A-4Q 0664/3-A-211 in 1972. This aircraft was lost in an accident five years later.

A-4Q aircraft aboard the aircraft carrier ARA *25 de Mayo* in the first A-4Q embarkation in October 1972.

Four Skyhawks from the 3rd Naval Attack Squadron, along with two Alouette III helicopters from the 1st Naval Helicopter Squadron, aboard ARA *25 de Mayo* in the early stages of the A-4s' operational career.

Skyhawk 0659/A-206 photographed between 1972 and 1973.

A-4Q A-213 about to trap the arrester wire aboard ARA *25 de Mayo*.

A-4Q 0666/3-A-213 which was lost in an accident on the aircraft carrier on 13 June 1975.

The A-4Qs were the first jets to operate regularly on aircraft carriers in Argentina. Previously only a Grumman Panther had made an arrested landing on the ARA *Independencia*.

Chapter 2

Almost War, the Conflict with Chile

Lieutenant Commander Rodolfo Castro Fox, C.O. of the 3rd Fighter and Attack Squadron during the Falklands War, explains his participation in this previous crisis:

> I had forgotten about the noise produced by an internal combustion engine as opposed to a jet engine and on the first take-off to adapt the T-28 to the School, in the middle of the race I asked the then Lieutenant Commander Jorge Paris, who was flying as safety pilot from the rear seat, if the noise it was making was normal. 'No,' he replied, 'Abort the take-off, the engine is failing!' I braked the plane a few metres from the end of the runway. As Head of the Air Instruction Department, my main responsibility was the development of the flying courses and I was in charge of the planning, the fulfilment of the programme and the verification of the levels obtained. I soon began to fly with each of the instructors to check the standardisation of the flight procedures and later to carry out periods with the students to follow the development of the instruction and later to carry out the in-flight examinations for their first 'solo' in the T-28. It was the last year of the 'Fennec'; it would soon be replaced by the Beech T-34-C-1 Turbo Mentor recently acquired for training at the School. For the flight transfer of the T-34s from the United States, a commission had been formed and arrived in June with the first eight aircraft out of a total of fifteen. The second commission, with the exception of the transfer chief, was to be carried out by the group of pilots who had been instructing during that period, including myself. Having flown the T-34 during July and part of August, in mid-August we left aboard a Navy Lockhead Electra L-188, eight pilots – one more than the number of aircraft to be transferred, in case the need for a replacement arose – and a group of mechanics to provide logistical support for the transfer.
>
> At the Beech Aircraft Corporation factory in Wichita, Kansas, we conducted acceptance flights and within a week began moving the aircraft into the country. Powered by a 715hp Pratt & Whitney PT-6A-25 turboprop engine and equipped with a three-bladed beta pitch propeller, this trainer was very reliable. It had oxygen and, although it did not have a pressurized cabin, transfer flight levels would be between 13,000 and 17,000ft, with an acceptable airspeed and a good range thanks to its fuel load. On the first day of the transfer, we flew over the entire North American territory from Wichita to the Mexican border, with a technical stopover and in five hours of flight time. According to Mexican government regulations, no more than four military aircraft could fly over their territory simultaneously or in a four-day period, so the next day, from a comfortable hotel in Brownsville, we saw the division

of Lieutenant Commander Jorge Paris, head of the transfer commission, depart for Veracruz. Four days later, the division of the three remaining planes under my command would land in El Salvador, after almost six hours of flight with a technical stopover in Veracruz for refuelling. Our flight would not have the same incidents as the previous one, which for meteorological reasons had to land in Guatemala in the midst of a political-military upheaval in that country and under threat of weapons had to clarify its origin and destination, totally oblivious to the events that were taking place. Once again, with the two divisions reunited in El Salvador, we completed the stage to San José, Costa Rica and another trip to Panama. We were supported by the L-188, which not only carried mechanics and spare parts, but also kept us abreast of weather information by radio in that unstable area. This would be very useful on the next leg to Guayaquil, a flight of more than five hours with a technical stop. We would then stop in Lima, where we would find the traditional hospitality of the Peruvian Naval Aviation, in whose origins, in the training of fixed-wing pilots, I had participated in 1965, as a flight instructor at the Naval Aviation School, meeting again with those pilots who had already reached the highest ranks, and we would take three days to carry out the corresponding maintenance inspections for 25 hours of flight time for the aircraft and for the crews to rest. The situation with Chile, so deteriorated in 1978, determined that we would avoid flying over it. We therefore flew from Lima to Tacna, in southern Peru, and from there, the next day, we would cross the Andes Mountains to Santa Cruz de la Sierra, in Bolivia. The level of the airway required us to climb to 26,000ft and although there were no problems with oxygen, flying without a pressurized cabin at that level was very uncomfortable, we felt swollen like sponges, the dilation of the body's organs was evident and the journey at that level was not a short one. We would enter the country through Jujuy International Airport and from there we would fly the same day to Corrientes. On 14 September we covered the Corrientes–Punta Indio leg, landing after almost a month's absence, with a journey of more than two weeks and 35 hours of flight time. Our families and an unpleasant surprise awaited us; in two hours we were to take off for the Espora Base to take part in an important parade over Puerto Belgrano the following day. Now I don't remember what the important reason was, but I do remember the lack of consideration they showed us.

In October I was summoned to Espora for a stage aboard the aircraft carrier *25 de Mayo* to crew the A-4Q. After taking my theoretical exams on aircraft knowledge and operation, and with only three and a half hours of PTAP flying time, in two days I made eight hook-ups and returned to give instruction in the T-28 to the School. The situation in the Beagle Channel Islands was the reason for this instruction; also at Punta Indio we were working on the possible deployment to the southern airfields with the T-34 and T-28 of the School and the Macchi of the 1st Naval Air Attack Squadron, as well as the remaining reconnaissance and liaison aircraft. While we continued to give flying instruction to the students, we practiced combat and firing manoeuvres with the instructors on the firing range. In early December, while the squadrons from Punta Indio were detached to the Big Island of Tierra del Fuego, I was ordered to report to the 3rd Fighter Attack Squadron to join the carrier strike group with the Skyhawk. Again I did three hours flying time and on 8 December I was attached to the ship. The Air Strike Group was at the peak of its operational capability, with eleven A-4Qs and seventeen pilots, plus a signal officer, Lieutenant Axel Adlercreuts, called up from a commercial airline he had joined after applying shortly before for retirement from the Navy. He was not the only call-up among the retired personnel, and several had spontaneously jumped at the chance to serve on the occasion. Some former chiefs among them were assigned to fill positions at the Bases where the pilots were leaving to deploy to the theatre of operations. As we sailed south, the pilots conducted training flights and weapon system tuning. During the development of the so-called 'Operation Thunderer' the planes were kept in a state of maximum alert and with ILC (Interceptor Ready on Deck) in conditions to be catapulted in a few minutes and armed with two AIM-9B 'Sidewinder' missiles and 20mm cannon. To cover this watch we had to carry out routine tests on the aircraft, and then remain on board for two hours ready to start and be catapulted immediately. In this case we only had one sub-wing fuel tank – the ventral one – and most of the time, because of the distance we were operating in the east of Staten Island, we had no way of getting to an alternative airfield on the ground if we were unable to hook up. For this reason there were A-4Q aircraft ready with Sargent Fletcher 'Buddy Pack' in-flight refuelling tanks at the belly station ready to meet the aircraft in trouble to transfer fuel to it in flight. Thanks to this foresight we also covered the watch of the 'Tanker', the aircraft equipped with this system. In these conditions, with the sub-wing tanks and the 'Buddy Pack', we were catapulted with the maximum weight of 22,500lbs, which required a catapult acceleration that left the aircraft with 150 knots (280km/h) flying forward. A real 'push' at the rear to reach this speed in 45m of travel, starting from about 40km/h (the speed of the aircraft). It was the turn of the Squadron Commander, the then Lieutenant Commander Julio I. Lavezzo made the first interception on 21 December of a Chilean Navy CASA 212 aircraft. This scout plane had taken off from Puerto Williams and was searching east of Isla de los Estados for the position of our fleet. The High Command did not authorize it to be shot down and, after receiving intimidating passes and failing to establish radio contact, the reconnaissance aircraft opted to withdraw to the mainland. There were also false alarms with unidentified aircraft of our own, but on another occasion a CASA 212 was intercepted again and the A-4Q action was repeated, this time manned by Lieutenant Horacio Pettinari, who also did not have authorization to shoot it down. These encounters were the climax of the actions from the sea. A few hours before the planned landing operations were due to take place, the ship and her escorts set a northerly course following orders from the High Command. The Pope's mediation halted the operation. On 24 December, we stood out with the aircraft carrier's planes in the vicinity of the Gulf of San Matias, heading for Espora. There we celebrated Christmas Eve with the group of Air Force pilots who were deployed at the base, but in my case, 700km away from Stella and the boys. I continued at Espora until mid-January flying the A-4Q, until the situation left no doubt that we were moving from 'almost war' to peaceful negotiation.

By the end of January I was flying the T-28 and T-34 again at the Naval Aviation School, continuing my task as head of the Air Instruction Department, now with the rank of Lieutenant Commander. During that year 1979, student training would begin with the T-34-C-1; the T-28s were decommissioned and nine of them were transferred to the Uruguayan Naval Aviation. For advanced training, the Beech Aircraft Super King Air 200 was incorporated, equipped with two 850 SHP Pratt & Whitney PT-6A-41 turboprop engines and three-bladed reversible pitch propellers. This short-range transport aircraft, with a maximum weight of 5,670kg, equipped with modern instruments, was a good multi-engine school, and in it I had my first contact with the flight director, the autopilot associated with it and the colour weather radar. On 25 June, on one of the many training flights, I had my first incident with a T-34, 1-A-415. It corresponded to the Precision stage and was the verification of a student of the Prefectura Naval Argentina, the assistant officer Eduardo Jireck. First we had practiced five precision landings over Punta Indio and then we completed the period with two-turn turns in one of the work zones. The power applied was that corresponding to aerobatics (950p/lbs of torque). After the fifth turn and in level flight, the torque, flowmeter and gas turbine revolutions (N1) indications started to fluctuate. I took control of the aircraft, reduced the torque for level flight (600p/lbs of torque) and at 8,500ft I headed towards the Base with the intention of making a precautionary approach, declaring the emergency as a priority on the circuit. The failure was getting worse and near the airfield the power drop was considerable. In these conditions, with low power and cruise propeller pitch, at optimum glide speed, the altitude loss had greatly increased approaching 1,000ft per minute and I decided to mark the propeller for improvement. The T-34 had become a glider, only its L/D (lift to drag ratio) was small and it maintained the descent between 500/700ft per minute. At the head of the runway, flying from the rear cockpit, I started the emergency approach, which by custom of the simulated demonstrations, was indicating to the student who in the front cockpit followed the manoeuvres that I was carrying out to comply with the altitude and speed parameters that would ensure me the first third of the runway for the touchdown. The operation of the landing gear and flap, operated by electrical circuits, was normal, as was the landing, although the aircraft was going a little faster than normal because the propeller could not apply the beta pitch, which increases drag and aids braking, due to the propeller being on the flag. The emergency had originated in the failure of a small piece of Teflon inside the turbine's fuel control unit, which restricted fuel flow. To my delight, months later, I read a modification to the aircraft manufacturer's flight procedures manual, which recommended, in cases of power loss below 400p/lbs of torque, to apply the flag pitch to improve the descent ratio. My decision, based on experience, had been correct. That year, the Inter-Forces Shooting Tournament would be held during the month of October at the Río Grande Naval Air Base, and the School would participate for the first time with the T-34-C-1 aircraft. We would stand out a week before with the so-called Grupo Aeronaval Insular to operate previously in the Isla Grande de Tierra del Fuego from its Field Aerodromes, developed in 1978 by the Beagle Channel case. These were dirt runways or sectors of asphalt road in different parts of the island, where aircraft such as the T-28 or T-34 could operate with limitations in case of deployment. That week we would do so at the eastern head of Lake Fagnano, where a short grass runway surrounded by mountains and next to the lake would be the place of operations. We slept in underground shelters, dug out and with covered access so as not to be identified, and the cold was combated with wood stoves made from 200-litre jerry cans. It was burned inside the pit, and there was a hidden pipe so that the smoke could escape to the outside, although much of it stayed inside. The toilet was handmade, our own creation, also with jerry cans, and melt water was what we used to wash ourselves. To prepare food we had a field kitchen and the menu didn't vary much: stews or noodles. We received orders to carry out certain missions by radio and some of them were carried out by taking off at night with a beacon provided by paraffin canisters and the knowledge we had acquired of the mountains around us for the departure routes. We refuelled in the 'Pillow-Tanks', field fuel tanks from which – by means of manual pumps and passing it through special filters to avoid contamination – we transferred the aero-kerosene to the aircraft. When we arrived at the Río Grande Base after a week in those conditions, the first thing we noticed was the disgusted look on the faces of those who had been operating from that base when they welcomed us: we had been smoking and without showers for days, and we looked like lepers from the way we were being led around. In those days a hot shower had been our greatest wish. In the Shooting Tournament we could only compete in glide and glide bombing, as the T-34 then lacked machine gun pods and had not yet been equipped with a rocket launching system. For this reason, a discussion arose as to whether our participation would be valid to compete for the Championship, which was the sum of several events. The A-4Q and Macchi squadrons of that year would also perform night bomb drops. We had not practiced it at the School because it was a shooting condition not foreseen for us. I had no choice but to challenge that we would also participate in night bombing, so we would do four tests out of six, including tactical navigation. The smiles from the trained attack pilots of the intervening squadrons ranged from mocking to sympathetic, but the challenge was accepted. That night three of us went out to practice night take-off in T-34s for the first time, and although the three pilots, then Navy Lieutenant Luis Collavino, Frigate Lieutenant Owen Crippa and I had done it in other aircraft, this time it would be with a 45-degree dive, because with less glide angle the necessary sight corrections were obscured by the long engine of the aircraft and therefore, to see where to aim, a sharper dive had to be made for less correction. The test experience was not very satisfactory, but it was important for the following night's tournament. We competed with Lieutenant Collavino and on the first shot I was lucky enough to find the correct firing parameters that repeated my numeral. Some people told us afterwards that we were above the minimum recovery height because we were launching too low at 45 degrees, but at night it is difficult to see the aircraft on the Arpa (abacus-like system for measuring launch parameters from the ground control station) and we repeated the four launches, each with remarkable results. The next day, when I received the award for winning the test individually, there were no more smiles on the faces of the pilots of the other squadrons. It wasn't enough to win the tournament, but we didn't lose out in the overall results. At the end of the same month we made the final navigation with the students of the Naval Aviation School, flying over Cordoba, Mendoza, Neuquen, Bariloche and from there along the southern Atlantic coast to Río Grande and then back to Punta Indio, with more than 24 hours of air navigation in nine days. That month would add up to 65 hours of flying, and was not the highest of the year. Then came the advanced stage in multi-engine, flying the BE-200, to finish the course in December. In January I would prepare for the Naval War College entrance exam, which, according to Stella, I would not pass if they took into account my apparent dedication to study, as I used to study while sunbathing in the Base's swimming pool and my colour was not that of someone dedicated to books. But in February I entered the course I was to do for half a year. By the middle of 1980 I had again being posted to the 3rd Naval Fighter and Attack Squadron. I had over 5,200 hours of flying experience, almost 1,600 of them as an instructor, and had made 216 carrier landings. This time we were travelling in a 1978 Renault 12 Break, which suited the family group.

T-28P 0580/3-A-226, c/n 174-652 ex USAF 51-7799, ex Armeé de l'Air 26, received in July 1966 and integrated in the 2nd Naval Air Squadron General Purpose as 0580/4-G-60, re-registered as 0580/3-A-226 in November 1968, decommissioned in 1979.

The Argentine Navy purchased from France a total of forty-five T-28Ps, modified with reinforced landing gear and arrester hook for carrier operations. (*Photo Sergio García Pedroche*)

The T-28 was replaced by the Beech T-34C-1 Turbo Mentor, although it was not carrier capable. During the Falklands War it was used as a light attack aircraft.

A Chilean Navy CASA C-212 Aviocar, like the one intercepted near the Beagle Channel.

Tercera Escuadrilla pilots at Comandante Espora Naval Air Station.

Commander Castro Fox (right) after his first flight late in 1981 after recovering from his injuries.

Commander Castro Fox, saluting his wingman.

Tercera Escuadrilla pilots aboard the carrier ARA *25 de Mayo* during the Chilean crisis.

An A-4Q prepares to trap on the deck of *25 de Mayo*.

Planes and helicopters on the deck of *25 de Mayo* during the deployment for landing on the Falkland Islands.

Eight A-4Qs photographed before the Falklands War.

Tercera Escuadrilla Aeronaval de Caza y Ataque A-4Q Skyhawks at Comandante Espora Naval Air Station.

Chapter 3

Top Cover for the Amphibious Landings

Due to the increased tension of the diplomatic conflict over South Georgia, on 23 March 1982 the Argentine Government met with the General Staff of the Command-in-Chief of the Navy to activate the plan carried out at the beginning of the year, now called Operation Blue (it was renamed Operation Rosario hours before landing). Three days later the order was given to carry out the operation on 1 April, with an alternative for the 2nd or 3rd of the same month and with time to stop it until 18:00 on 31 March.

On 28 March, the fleet left the Puerto Belgrano Naval Base, with a landing force to occupy the Falkland Islands, and the following day four Grumman S-2E Trackers (2-AS-22, 23, 25 and 26) of the Anti-submarine Naval Squadron and three A-4Q Skyhawks (3-A-301, 305 and 314) landed on the aircraft carrier *25 de Mayo*, en route to the south. The Sea King 2-H-234 and Alouette IIIs 3-H-105, 111 and 112 also arrived. In the days leading up to the landing, the Trackers made seven surveillance flights near the islands, finding no British ships, only around forty Polish and Russian fishing vessels. Due to a major storm on the night of 31 March to 1 April, the operation was delayed until 2 April.

The Argentine forces were organized into Amphibious Task Force 40 (FT40) commanded by Rear Admiral Gualter Allara, Coverage Task Force 20 (FT20) commanded by Captain José Sarcona and Aeronaval Task Force 80 (FT80) under the command of Rear Admiral Carlos García Boll.

The FT20 included the aircraft carrier *25 de Mayo* with its Embarked Air Group, the destroyers *Comodoro Py*, *Bouchard* and *Piedra Buena*, and the tanker *Punta Médanos*.

The FT80 was organized as follows:

GT80.1 Insular.
80.1.1 1st Naval Attack Squadron.
80.1.2 Naval Aviation School.
80.1.3 Aeronaval Reconnaissance Squadron.
80.1.4 General Purpose Naval Air Squadron.
80.1.5 Air Service of the Argentine Naval Prefecture.

GT80 Surveillance 2.
80.2.1 Naval Exploration Squadron.
80.2.2 Anti-submarine Naval Air Squadron.

GT80.3 Attack.
80.3.1 2nd Naval Fighter and Attack Squadron.
80.3.2 3rd Attack Naval Squadron.
80.3.3 1st Aeronaval Helicopter Squadron.

GT80.4 Mobile logistics support.
80.4.1 1st Aeronaval Squadron of Mobile Logistics Support.
80.4.2 2nd Aeronaval Squadron of Mobile Logistics Support.

Naval Aviation would be organized as the Embarked Air Group, and a Coastal Air Group with the Exploration Task Unit with two SP-2H Neptunes, one Beechcraft B-200 and two Lockheed Electras. Also this group would have the Attack Task Unit, with three A-4Qs, seven Aermacchi MB-326s and six to eight MB-339s, a squadron of FAA Mirage IIIEAs and one of IAI M5 Daggers, but only one squadron of Mirages was actually deployed. The Medical Services Task Unit was also organized, with two Electras and three Fokker F-28s.

In the end, the attack aviation was not used during the landing and, after that, the A-4Qs embarked on the aircraft carrier returned to their base on 6 April and the squadron began to carry out the necessary training to achieve the greatest effectiveness and professionalism of its operations. Five A-4Q pilots who were stationed outside the unit were incorporated, as well as five more aircraft, totalling eight aircraft, the maximum possible at the time. In-flight refuelling practice were conducted with an FAA KC-130H, alongside the Super Étendards. With the help of the S-2 Tracker as scouts/pathfinders, attacks on surface units were simulated, such as Type 42 destroyers (ARA *Hercules* and *Santísima Trinidad*) that were similar to the Royal Navy ones. During these tests they concluded that they should approach a height of less than 500ft within 100 nautical miles, less than 100ft within 50 nautical miles and finally less than 50ft when within 30 nautical miles of the ship to avoid radar detection. Once in visual range, they had to carry out manoeuvres to avoid cannon fire and pass over the ship with a separation greater than 20 seconds, to avoid being affected by the explosions of the bombs of the previous planes. At that time jets 3-A-301 and 306 received Omega VLF equipment, while in two others sonobuoy receivers were tested, to experience the guiding of squadrons by means of sonobuoys launched by the Trackers, using them as a VOR.

On 18 April the squadron embarked on *25 de Mayo* with twelve pilots and eight aircraft. During the voyage, a deck-ready interceptor guard (ILC) was mounted, with two five-minute catapult aircraft armed with AIM-9B Sidewinder missiles, as well as another anti-surface attack division with four aircraft in bomber configuration (six Mk 82) and a chaff-launching plane, all on 30 minutes' standby. The eighth aircraft, 3-A-302, was configured as a tanker, equipped with the Buddy Pack. When the guard sections were launched and due to the lack of an alternative aerodrome, the tanker aircraft was kept in flight.

After disembarking, the ships were organized into Task Force 79, with Task Group 79.1 formed by the aircraft carrier and 79.2 by their escort, with the destroyers ARA *Hercules*, *Santísima Trinidad*, *Seguí* and *Comodoro Py*, and the tanker *Punta Médanos*. The rest of the warships formed Task Groups 79.3 and 79.4 that operated separately.

Between the day they embarked and until 27 April, surveillances were carried out in the northern part of the Falklands. The following day, FT.79 was ordered to remain a diversified potential threat, to operate on an opportune basis, so on the 29th the FT.79 commander ordered the Task Groups to locate near the Total Exclusion Zone set by the British.

On 30 April, information was received on the proximity of the British task force, so it was ordered to relocate to the north-west of the Falklands.

At 15:13 on 1 May, Tracker 2-AS-23 obtained contact with seven targets that it considered to be the British fleet in position 49º34' S / 57º10' W. Minutes later, at 15:30 echoes were detected of aircraft on radar and the interceptor section was launched, which found the FAA Canberras returning from their attempt to attack the British fleet.

Faced with this reality, it was decided to carry out an attack on the British fleet with the Skyhawks. Naval Aviation concluded that, according to the probability tables and considering the British anti-aircraft defences, of the six planes that took off (carrying twenty-four bombs), only four were able to launch (sixteen bombs) and returned to the aircraft carrier two aircraft. Of the sixteen bombs dropped, there was a 25 per cent probability of impact, which was enough to neutralize a ship. At 05:28, another Tracker went out to determine the position of the fleet before an attack with the Skyhawks was launched, although it had problems with its radar. After seeing the Russian fishing boats move away, they detected a very powerful radar emission among them. Although they flew over the formation, they could not see the ship that was emitting, although it was evident that there was a ship nearby acting as a radar picket. Then they flew a little further east, failing to detect the British ships.

The planes were prepared and the pilots Lieutenant Commander Philippi, Lieutenants Márquez, Olmedo, Arca and Lecour and Ensign Médici were on guard duty. The distance between the two fleets at the time was more than 200 miles, above the range of the Skyhawk with the armament they carried, which was 150 miles. Although the aircraft carrier began to approach, there was no time to position herself before sunset, which was at 18:00, since the A-4Qs did not operate at night.

At 18:00 the FT.79 withdrew to the south, maintaining a zig-zag while waiting for a new exploration. At night Tracker 2-AS-26 was sent out, which made contact with the enemy fleet at 23:00, now in position 50º00' S / 56º25' W.

Meanwhile, the planes were being prepared with the new pilots on duty, leaving 3-A-301 with Lieutenant Commander Castro Fox, 3-A-114 with Lieutenant Márquez, 3-A-302 with Lieutenant Benítez, 3 -A-306 with Lieutenant Oliveira, 3-A-312 with Lieutenant Lecour and 3-A-305 with Lieutenant Sylvester. Another aircraft would remain in reserve and one as a refuelling tanker, should the need arise.

The planes were scheduled to be launched at 06:00 on 2 May, although a new exploration could not find the enemy ships. Although the attack with the A-4Qs was intended to be the same, there were only 10 knots of wind and 40 knots of relative wind (wind plus ship speed) were needed to launch the aircraft with their load of fuel and bombs. This was unusual in the South Atlantic and ultimately prevented what would be the first aircraft carrier to aircraft carrier encounter since the Second World War. It is also necessary to add the precarious state of the aircraft carrier's catapult, which required there to be a lot of head wind, which also imposed constant change of course.

While the two interceptors were kept on five-minute alert and the six bombers to 30 minutes from take-off. At 9:00 a red alert was issued by unidentified aircraft and 3-A-304 was catapulted with Lieutenant Commander Philippi, although 3-A-307 with Ensign Médici was unable to do so due to failures. At 11:00 there was another alarm and 3-A-307 was launched, having been repaired, with Lieutenant Márquez and 3-A-304 with Lieutenant Commander Castro Fox. However, it was estimated that the alarms were Air Force planes that returned to the continent.

Due to the sinking of the cruiser ARA *General Belgrano* (C-4) and the failure to detect British ships, the attack was suspended. On the morning of 3 May, the two interceptors were kept on five-minute alert (3-A-304 and 307) with the pilots in one-and-a-half-hour shifts and the six surface-attack aircraft (3-A- 301, 302, 305, 306, 312 and 314) with the pilots on duty for three hours.

At 13:30 the order to withdraw the aircraft carrier arrived, since it was supposed to be attacked at any time by the submarine HMS *Spartan*. However, according to Admiral Woodward, the English nuclear submarine at that time was unable to locate the carrier. Subsequently, Task Group 79.1 remained near the coast, waiting for a favourable opportunity to act against the enemy. After the withdrawal, only two interceptor sections remained, with aircraft 3-A-304, 307, 312 and 314, leaving the other four configured for attack. In the afternoon there was a new alarm and 3-A-304 with Lieutenant Commander Philippi and 3-A-307 with Ensign Médici were launched, although they were again Air Force planes. On the last shift of the day, aircraft 3-A-304 (Lieutenant Commander Zubizarreta), 3-A-307 (Lieutenant Olmedo) and 3-A-314 (Lieutenant Lecour) were catapulted, with the same result. During the following days, a single section of interceptors was kept on alert, as the ship moved away from the combat zone.

On 9 May, the Skyhawks were landed in Puerto Belgrano and on the 12th they were sent to the Rear Admiral Quijada Aeronaval Base in Río Grande to operate from there. However, four aircraft returned to Espora due to problems and two flew the following day, completing the unit on 14 May.

From the following day, six aircraft were maintained in attack configuration with four 250kg Mk 82 Snakeye bombs, plus one reserve and a tanker. Two divisions were organized with the following pilots: 1st Division: Lieutenant Commander Castro Fox, Ensign Médici, Lieutenant Benitez, Lieutenant Commander Zubizarreta, Lieutenants Olmedo and Oliveira. Second Division: Lieutenant Commander Philippi, Lieutenants Márquez, Arca, Rótolo Lecour and Sylvester.

On 18 May, due to an accident, the Buddy Pack on 3-A-302 broke down, leaving the unit unable to refuel in flight, for which it was necessary to rely exclusively on the KC-

130H of the Air Force. The plane was repaired two days later, although the Buddy Pack would not in the end be used in combat operations.

The following day, to evaluate the possibility of operating in conjunction with the Super Étendards, a flight was made between two A-4Qs with Lieutenant Commander Philippi and Ensign Médici and a Super Étendard, with Lieutenant Commander Curilovic.

A-4Qs 3-A-304 and 3-A-308 aboard *25 de Mayo*.

Mixed formation shortly before the war, with 3-A-301 alongside the Aermacchi MB-326GB 0647/4-A-108 and the Beech T-34C1 0722/1-A-404.

A-4Q 3-A-308 was the only A-4Q to survive the war without receiving camouflage. 3-A-306 only carried it for a short time, as it was lost in an accident on 16 December 1982.

A-4Q 3-A-306, 309 and 304 aboard *25 de Mayo* during the Fraternal IV exercise with Brazil in October 1982.

A-4Q 3-A-301 catapulted from the aircraft carrier. The strobe that has just been released from the Skyhawk at the end of the catapult run can be seen.

Chapter 4

Naval Aviation Skyhawks in Combat

Throughout its 18-year history Tercera Escuadrilla Aeronaval de Caza y Ataque had a very important commitment to close air support (CAS) for amphibious operations carried out by the marines. Secondly came anti-shipping strikes and daylight interceptions, the Skyhawks carrying a pair of AIM-9B Sidewinders for the latter role. 3ª Escuadrilla created a new tactical doctrine in Argentine Naval Aviation and in 1981 2ª Escuadrilla Aeronaval de Caza y Ataque was reformed with Super Étendards. 3ª Escuadrilla became the supplier of pilots for the Super Étendard unit and after the Falklands conflict worked also as an operational training unit, qualifying pilots in fast jet and carrier operations. Late in 1987, due to scarcity of aircraft – there were only five A-4Qs available, 3-A-301, -302, -304, -308 and -309 – the unit disbanded, although these Skyhawks continued flying for about six months more, until finally being phased out of service and withdrawn from the inventory. The last A-4Q flight was by aircraft 3-A-302 in April 1988.

The Falklands War

In March 1982 3ª Escuadrilla comprised ten A-4Qs – three equipped with VLF-Omega navigation systems, 3-A-301, -306 and -309 – of which eight were operational. Shore based at Comandante Espora Naval Air Station, it formed part of 3ª Escuadra Aeronaval (3rd Naval Air Wing), frequently deploying aboard the Argentine Navy's only carrier ARA *25 de Mayo*. Twelve pilots were on strength: Lieutenant Commanders Castro Fox (CO), Zubizarreta (exec) and Philippi; Lieutenants Lecour, Sylvester, Arca, Benitez, Oliveira and Rótolo and Sub Lieutenants Márquez, Olmedo and Médici. The Escuadrilla received orders to embark its eight available Skyhawks aboard the *25 de Mayo* for scheduled exercises in the second half of March and on the 28th the ship weighed anchor as flagship of Task Force 20 (Fuerza de Tareas 20).

The unit's mission in 'Operacion Azul' (codename for the amphibious landings near Port Stanley) was to provide cover for the assault forces, Amphibious Task Force 40. Lack of British airborne opposition made it unnecessary to use the A-4Qs, although one was seen some days after the 2 April occupation operating from Port Stanley airfield, performing trials in case they could be forward-deployed there, but the runway proved too short for safe operations, especially with a war load and in wet or icy conditions. On 2 May 1982, the day after the first RAF/Fleet Air Arm raids over the Falklands, the fleets of both countries were on the verge of a classic World War Two-type action with the Argentine Task Force sailing northwest of the Falklands. This was the only time that such an opportunity existed and had an engagement taken place, the course of the war could have been quite different. That day the Skyhawks were in a high state of readiness, seven loaded with six Mk 82 Snakeye bombs for a possible strike against the Royal Navy carriers. The remaining A-4Q was kept in air defence mode armed with two AIM-9Bs, one centreline drop tank and the pilot in cockpit readiness. During the day orders to launch the bombers were cancelled at the last minute at least three times. Officially these cancellations were due to lack of wind which made catapult launch with heavy bomb and fuel load a marginal affair, and in any case the position of the Royal Navy warships had moved to the east. Before returning to port on 5 May, 3ª Escuadrilla made nine air defence sorties from the carrier, trying to intercept radar 'blips' detected by the Argentine Navy's Type 42 destroyers. No visual contact was made. On 9 May the eight serviceable A-4Qs deployed to Río Grande Naval Air Station in the Tierra del Fuego area, being joined later by the two other Skyhawks which had been put back into operational status.

From this southerly base, the Escuadrilla performed a total of thirty attack and armed reconnaissance sorties, engaging in combat during nine of them. The relative small number of engagements was due to the great mobility of naval targets, coupled with the considerable distance between Río Grande and the theatre of operations and worsened by the almost total lack of reconnaissance and intelligence-gathering means. In addition very poor weather conditions over the operations area and at Río Grande caused a good number of sorties to be aborted, among them the last one flown by the Escuadrilla on 12 June.

Three aircraft and two pilots were lost during operations (one in an accident). But they caused telling damage that led to the sinking of two Type 21 frigates. These successes were, and are still, hotly disputed by the Fuerza Aérea, which claims that its Skyhawk and Dagger flights were responsible.

In order that the reader could make a better judgement, the author obtained the following after-action reports from Aviacion Naval Headquarters, concerning the endeavours of 3ª Escuadrilla on 21 and 23 May, while Capitán de Corbeta (Lieutenant Commander) Alberto Jorge Philippi, leader of the ill-fated 'Tábano' (Horsefly) division which attacked the frigate HMS *Ardent* provides a dramatic account of his experiences, as well as one of his wingmen, Teniente de Navío (Lieutenant) José Cesar Arca, the only survivors of that mission.

MISSION REPORT

Day: 21 May 1982
Time: 15:01 Argentine (Zulu less 3).
Target: Type 21 Frigate located two miles to the north of Northeast Island in Falkland Sound.

Composition of Attack Force
1st Division
3-A-307 Lieutenant Commander Alberto Jorge Philippi
3-A-312 Lieutenant Jose Cesar Arca
3-A-314 Sub Lieutenant Gustavo Marcelo Márquez.

2nd Division
3-A-301 Lieutenant Benito Italo Rótolo
3-A-305 Lieutenant Carlos Lecour
3-A-306 Lieutenant Roberto Sylvester
Stores and armament configuration
4 Mk 82 Snakeye 500lb retarded bombs per aircraft.
200 20mm HEI rounds per aircraft.
2 x 300-US gallon drop tanks per a/c.

Strike tactical procedures:
= Low level approach (less than 50ft).
= Climb to 300ft during attack leg.
= Dropping bombs with 250-millisecond intervals.
= Angle of separation among each attacking aircraft, approximately 30 degrees.

Chronology:
14:08: First Division (307, 312, 314) launched from Río Grande Naval Air Station.
14:25: Second Division (301, 305, 306) launched from Río Grande Naval Air Station.
14:50: First Division starts descent for low-level leg.
15:01: First Division attacks Type 21 frigate in Falkland Sound, near Northwest Island and Grantham Sound.
15:05: First division is intercepted by Sea Harriers during its escape. Two aircraft (314 and 307) are immediately shot down, while the third (312) is abandoned by its pilot due to damage from 30mm gunfire.
15:30: Second division attacks Type 21 frigate in San Carlos Sound beside Port San Carlos; escape as briefed.
16:40: Second division lands at Río Grande.

Notes: Both divisions had the same mission and launch time hour, but troubles with the Omega navigation systems of aircraft 305 and 306 forced the second to be launched 17 minutes after the first, continuing its attack independently.

MISSION REPORT
Day: 23 May 1982
Time: 14:09 Argentine official (Zulu less 3)
Target: Type 21 frigate detected in San Carlos Water.

Composition of attack force
3-A-301 Lieutenant Commander Rodolfo Alberto Castro Fox
3-A-302 Lieutenant Marcos Benitez
3-A-306 Lieutenant Commander Carlos Zubizarreta
3-A-305 Lieutenant Carlos Oliveira

Stores and armament configuration:
Same as 21 May mission.

Strike tactical procedures:
Same as 21 May mission.

Chronology:
12:35: Division launched from Río Grande naval air station.
13:20: Air-to-air refuelling from Fuerza Aérea KC-130H tankers at 52 degrees 30 minutes S, 64 degrees W.
13:25: 3-A-305 returns to Río Grande due to technical malfunction in the refuelling probe transfer system, landing at 14:00 at Río Grande.
13:50: 3-A-301, 302 and 306 enter the operations area.
14:09: Visual detection of targets and attack.
15:15: 302 and 306 land at Río Grande.
15:30: 301 lands at Río Grande.

Notes: Aircraft 301, flown by the Escuadrilla CO, Lieutenant Commander Castro Fox, suffered fuel problems. After launching its bombs and while jinking to avoid AAA/SAM fire, one of the drop tanks ceased to transfer fuel to the main fuselage tank. Efforts to correct the failure were unsuccessful so he had to separate from his wingman, radioing them to return independently to Río Grande.

Castro Fox aborted the low-level escape leg, jettisoning all external stores and performing a high-angle climb profile (fouled deck range) as recommended by the NATOPS manual. He landed at Río Grande with only 200lbs of fuel remaining, having flown 380 nautical miles in marginal weather with a single-engined aircraft over the desolate and terribly cold South Atlantic Ocean.

Lieutenant Commander Carlos Zubizarreta, number three in the division, had an electrical failure and could not launch his bombs.

The other twenty combat sorties flown by the Escuadrilla from Río Grande were as follows.

On 21 May, two three-aircraft divisions led by Lieutenant Commanders Castro Fox and Zubizarreta were launched at 10:15 for attacking British shipping in Falkland Sound, bad weather forced the cancellation of the mission which returned at 12:30. On 26 May Lieutenants Olmedo (in 301) and Médici (in 302) launched at 09:27 for an armed recce mission over West Falkland, no contact was made and the section landed at 11:17. A similar mission, again unsuccessful, was launched next day, this time aircraft 301 was flown by Lieutenant Oliveira and 302 by Lieutenant Olmedo, the section took off at 09:20 and landed at 11:05. On 28 May an anti-shipping strike was planned in Falkland Sound area, the mission included air-to-air refuelling, the section launched at 11:15 and was formed by Lieutenant Sylvester in 301 and Lieutenant Lecour in 302, no contact was established and the pair landed at Río Grande at 13:05. The next combat mission over the islands did not take place until ten days later. On 8 June Lieutenant Oliveira in 301 and Lieutenant Olmedo in 305 were briefed to attack ground positions in Broken Island, Skyhawks refuelled from an KC-130H en route, each aircraft dropped four Mk 82 at 14:04, landing at Río Grande at 10:47. Next day Lieutenant Rótolo in 301 and Médici in 302 were briefed for an armed recce and targets of opportunity attack in the Fitzroy area, with AAR en route, the pair launched at 13:35, but near the target area, a Sea Harrier CAP was detected, the section making good their escape and landed at 15:45. The last 3ª Escuadrilla combat sortie of the war was on 12 June 1982, it was an armed recce mission over the east coast of East Falkland Island, near Bouganville Island, the Skyhawks were 3-A-301 with Lieutenant Rótolo at the controls and 3-A-302 with Lieutenant Médici, each one carrying four Mk 82s, the section was launched at 13:45, refuelling from a KC-130H Hercules from Grupo 1 de Transporte en route. Weather over the operations area was very bad, no contact with British shipping was established, and once the pair turned for the return leg, they flew near to a Sea Harrier CAP, all external loads were jettisoned and the Skyhawks accelerated to maximum speed. With minimum fuel both landed safely at Río Grande at 16:05.

Lieutenant Rótolo narrates that:

> When this mission was ordered, the A-4Qs refuelled and received the weapons to leave around 14:00, having to be fast due to the few hours of daylight. When we had the mission briefing, we were informed that there was a target that was probably a damaged transport in the southern part of the Falklands Strait. The idea was to hit the target, bomb it, and try to sink it; also if we found other objectives, that we do the same.
>
> Minutes later, while we were putting on our flight suits, the command informed us that the ship was not alone and that it perhaps had two or three companions. Later, while we were inspecting the plane before departure, new information arrived: there was no transportation, what we would find were many units of the Royal Navy that support the landing of ground troops and our mission was to attack the first ship that we found in the area of operations.
>
> An S-2E Tracker aircraft, on reconnaissance near the area, south of the San Carlos Strait, was supposed to guide us to the target. We did not have time to organize in-flight refuelling, so we would operate at the range limit. But we had to do the mission anyway because that day the British were landing in San Carlos and we had to attack as soon as possible.
>
> Take-off was normal, despite the conditions of the Río Grande runway. It was better than doing it on an aircraft carrier, but it was marginal anyway. Everything worked normally. we flew 10 minutes apart from the other three planes. We could not accelerate too far to reach them because we had to take care of the fuel because the reserve to return home was small and we always thought about the alternative of being damaged by enemy 20mm or 30mm shots, piercing the fuel tanks. Because of this, it was not easy to think of a safe return.

Because the Tracker operated from a different aerodrome than ours, due to a misunderstanding, we did not agree at the time of reaching the target and had no contact with it before the attack. When we were close to beginning the descent, 100 miles from the islands, flying at 30,000ft, we heard some communications from the other group, who were inside the strait at the time. The information they gave us was that the small islands we saw on the maps were low, so we couldn't hide behind them to avoid being detected by enemy radars. We were also told that the ship that had to be in the southern part of the San Carlos Strait was not there.

We started descending when we heard Lieutenant Márquez say that he had found a destroyer in the middle of the strait. Captain Philippi said 'attack him'. They attack the ship, we hear something else, until we finally hear Márquez say 'Harrier, Harrier' and later a voice that I think was from Lieutenant Commander Philippi saying 'I am ejecting', so we realized that the Harriers were there.

We had some options, but we decided to carry out the order to make the attack, but with the difference that, when we were very low and crossing the southern part of the strait, knowing that the small islands were not useful to hide from the radars of the ships, I told my colleagues that we would continue the mission despite the problems with the other section. I said that we would cross to the other coast to fly over Isla Soledad and avoid detection. With a very short communication I asked my colleagues if they were with me to do the mission and they answered affirmatively.

Finally we reach the Bay of Ruiz Puente and turn towards the sound. In that place, the coast enters the island and there we saw some boats, one in the centre of the can.

At that moment we started the attack. We realized that, against the other coast, within the canal, more ships were obscured by the shadows of the coast. It was a day with gusts, sun, rain, with spaces between the clouds and those ships opened fire on our course, which was perpendicular to the ship that was in the middle of the channel. The Type 21 frigate opened fire with machine guns and also the other ships. We saw the impacts in the water. We did the classic zigzag to avoid the point predicted by weapons systems, a not very effective defence, but it was the only thing we could do in those circumstances. We have to assume that the enemy, when it is firing, is also shocked and that was really useful for us, because they did not reach our planes, we also expected Sea Cat missiles, but they did not launch them.

We were going towards the target very close to the water and with a small separation between us, because there was no time to separate our planes to pass 20 seconds apart from the target, as established so that the numerals can avoid explosions from the bombs of the preceding plane. We had great skill at the time and good preparation in techniques and tactics against naval targets, so the moment I was going to pass over the ship I climbed 200ft, the height to enable the fins of the bombs have time to be armed and wishbones are ready to explode. Anyway, it seemed like it was too high for me, so after dropping the bombs I rotated the plane until it reversed to descend faster, somewhat normal at 10,000ft, and recovered very close to the water.

> Later I turned left to return south into the canal, but I found a 'County'-class destroyer in front of me (the *Antrim*), and it opened fire with all its weapons. I ordered my crew to turn my axis again, to the right, across the sound. While saying this, Sylvester and Lecour were dropping their bombs and I could see some of them. Anyway, they got the message and we escaped very low, almost touching the water, until we reached a hill above the coast. There we climb and hide behind it. While we were flying through some valleys, I asked my companions if they could see each other. Lecour was following me very close, but Sylvester was far away. At that moment we heard the voice of the Tracker pilot informing that he was ready to guide us, thinking that we were reaching the area of operations.
>
> The attack was very effective, we could not speak because the enemy could find our position, and the worst part was to come. To escape, we were forced to climb quickly to reduce fuel consumption, and feared that there might be a *Sheffield*-class destroyer in that area that could shoot down our aircraft with their Sea Dart missiles. We climb over the valleys and after passing the islands we reach 28,000 or 29,000ft. Once with the light aircraft, we could easily climb to 40,000ft, the limit of the Sea Dart. Without speaking, only with signs, we met and this was a very difficult moment. Very difficult because we became aware of what we had done.
>
> From the time we headed to the centre of the sound to make the attack until we started to climb, it took about five minutes. There were minutes under very high tension, although the firing was not much different from what we used to practice, with the exception of the separation between the planes, we had the additional ingredient of the psychological effect as a result of being under fire ... When we were about 150 miles from Río Grande we reported our return to base and asked about the pilots in the first section. They replied that they never returned. Calculating the elapsed time they no longer had enough fuel, so we confirmed that they had been shot down.
>
> About our attack, Lecour and Sylvester, who was the last in the bombardment, saw that two of my bombs passed over the ship and two were short. Lecour, with his bombs, had left the frigate surrounded by smoke and fire. This forced Sylvester to drop his bombs as he crossed the column of smoke produced by the bombs.
>
> Finally we arrived in Río Grande with so little fuel that we did not have the possibility of going around the airport. On the ground we become aware of what our baptism of fire was; we lost three pilots and three planes. Sylvester and Lecour's planes also had some hits.

In a meeting Rótolo had with Alan West, commander of HMS *Ardent* in 2000, West told him that both sections of the A-4Q hit the ship, and that the first one made two impacts, destroying the Sea Cat and damaging the stern. The second section made an impact (by Lecour) by exploding under the fuel tank, also at the stern. After that, West decided to head inshore and run the ship aground the ship to have time.

Two attack missions against naval targets were prepared for 22 May, each with two planes, which were cancelled by meteorology. However, the next day the A-4Qs would leave on a new mission, albeit a single squadron of four planes, with the fifth in reserve. First, an attack mission was prepared to a surface target that was sailing near the mainland, east of the Strait of Magellan, although a reconnaissance flight with the B-200 4-G-43 revealed that it was a merchant ship of its own. At 12:30 a new order arrived, to attack naval targets in Puerto San Carlos. The squadron included Lieutenant Commander Castro Fox (3-A-301), Lieutenant Commander Zubizarreta (3-A-306), Lieutenant Oliveira (3-A-305) and Lieutenant Benítez (3-A-302). They refuelled in flight from an Air Force KC-130 on the way to attack surface targets east of San Carlos. Oliveira suffered problems in the replenishment manoeuvre and had to return. The other three machines continued the mission. Lieutenant Benítez recalls that:

> As we passed Mount Rosalía sideways, with the bow towards the port, I was surprised by how high we were over the sound waters, I had to throw negative G to hit the water again and I saw that No. 1 He did the same, I was coming about 100 metres, behind and to the right and I stopped seeing number 3.
>
> Looking ahead I saw the ships, I could distinguish four, of which the ones on my right were warships, the leader made a small turn and pointed his plane at the largest and I appreciated that it was a 'County'-type destroyer [actually it was HMS *Intrepid* that when shooting a Sea Cat forced Castro Fox to make evasive manoeuvres when he dropped the bombs, causing them to miss], I pointed towards the fourth ship, which was a Type 21 frigate, they were very clear and they looked impeccable, there was no smoke, no fires, no trace of previous combat. When we reached the San Carlos arm, to our surprise, surface-to-air missiles began to fire from the ground. You could see the starting flashes and then they looked like red flares coming towards you slowly, one of them passed between the two planes; Closer to the ships the explosions of the anti-aircraft shells were seen and I noticed that the bow gun fired towards No. 1.
>
> When I saw that it was in the firing parameter for cannons, I pressed the trigger and instantly they locked, so I changed the selector and pressed the bombs, I felt the loss of the bombs and the nose tended to go up, I immediately turned 90° with a tilt of wings and I was heading north flush with the water to protect myself behind the mountains, at this moment a missile passed right in front of me and I thought that at any moment I would be shot down.

All the planes managed to escape, individually.

Castro Fox describes that 'initially it attacked a Type 21 frigate that was in the middle of the estuary, but I changed its target during the run when I saw it as more profitable. Next to launch, I had to make a sharp turn manoeuvre to avoid a Sea Cat missile launched from the bow of the ship. This affected my aim in the final part, and the launching of the bombs went beyond the target, my salvo being long.'

The ship attacked by Benítez was the frigate HMS *Antelope* that had also been damaged by an FAA A-4B and sank the following morning due to Argentine bombs. According to an investigation carried out by Castro Fox:

> After both airstrikes, the *Antelope* had two unexploded bomb hits and after transferring the crew to other units, its commander, Captain Nick Tobin, ordered the deactivation of the them. Different sources mention that they were two 500lb bombs and others that were 1,000lb. Regarding the one that was in the air-conditioning unit, on the two engine rooms near the starboard side, I have no doubt that it was the one dropped by the then First Lieutenant Luciano Guadagnini, hit by the anti-aircraft fire that caused him to collide with the stern mast and crash into the sea.

The second bomb that hit the ship penetrated the port bow, before the bridge and was lodged in the NCOs' mess. In the book *Our Falklands War*, by Geoffrey Underwood, statements by the ship's commander are transcribed, which he states regarding the first attack by two planes:

> A plane came directly at us. He dropped two bombs and was fired on by my starboard Oerlikon 20mm cannon, which was aimed and fired by Able Seaman 'Bunny' Warren. The plane was about 30ft above the water and was flying very fast. One bomb flew between the main mast and missed and the other hit the ship to starboard aft.
>
> The aircraft was hit by approximately eight shells from Warren's weapon. It stopped, hit the main mast, and disintegrated into a thousand pieces, scattering pieces about 100m from the ship.

Right after they were attacked by Navy planes,

> we opened fire with the 4.5in gun and the Seacat. The two planes turned and the Seacat missile pursued them through a nearby valley. We believe it destroyed the plane just above the ridge. Then we were attacked again from our side of the port and a bomb entered the ship in the vicinity of the NCO canteen. The attacks during which we were hit were carried out in approximately one minute and it was evident that they were coordinated and carried out in a very professional manner.

Two Army explosives experts, Warrant Officer Phillips and Staff Sergeant Jim Prescott, were dispatched to disarm the bombs. 'They were confident they would do the job,' said Captain Tobin.

> They started with the bomb aft and said they had only recently dealt with a similar one on another ship. It was late at night. They had made several attempts to defuse the bomb using various methods. It exploded during another attempt and cut a large hole in the side of the ship from the waterline to the funnel. Staff Sgt. Prescott died in the explosion and WO Phillips lost an arm.

This account would confirm that the bombs were different. As the explosives experts faced the disarmament of one they already knew (the Air Force used 1,000lb British-origin bombs and because of the long-delay fuze because they were low drag bombs when dropped on low-level flights, many of them did not explode on 21 May) and that the bow one was dropped by Lieutenant Benítez. It would also indicate that the origin of the first explosion would be during the attempt to defuse the bomb dropped by First Lieutenant Luciano Guadagnini.

Castro Fox attacked the *Intrepid* and his bombs fell into the water, according to a crew member of the ship, Martin Dunkin MEM (L) 1, 'something hit the ship, we never found out what hit the side. It could have been a bomb or part of an Argentine plane that was shot down over San Carlos, however when we returned to Portsmouth there were some holes in the side of the ship below the waterline, in one of our ballast tanks.' Therefore, the explosion in the water is likely to have caused the damage.

Back on the mainland, when Lieutenant Commander Zubizarreta landed, a main wheel tyre burst due to ice on the runway and the strong crosswind, his machine began to deviate from the runway, the nose train stop was cut and as he still had a bomb that had failed to drop, due to the likelihood of an explosion due to the fuze being armed, he ejected in a nose-down position without achieving a correct opening of his parachute. He died hours later in a Río Grande hospital.

The following day a guard was mounted with aircraft 3-A-301 (Lieutenant Oliveira) and 3-A-302 (Lieutenant Olmedo), although no mission was launched. On 25 May, an armed reconnaissance was planned over San Julían Bay, west of Gran Malvina, although it had to be cancelled again due to the meteorology in Río Grande. A day later, Lieutenant Olmedo in 3-A-301 and Lieutenant Médici in 3-A-302 made this flight between 9:27 and 11:17, without finding targets, so they returned to base. Upon landing, due to the wet runway 3-A-302 burst a tyre and had to snag on the cable at the end of the runway.

Another flight was completed at 12:37, when 3-A-301 with Lieutenant Rótolo and3-A-302 with Lieutenant Oliveira left to make an offensive reconnaissance of Bougainville Island. At 13:00 the KC-130 was seen but 3-A-301 had problems with an iced refuelling probe and both planes had to return, landing at 15:30.

A new armed reconnaissance was ordered on 27 May, when at 9:27 Lieutenant Oliveira left in 3-A-301 and Lieutenant Olmedo in 3-A-302, flying over Cabo Belgrano and Bahía San Julián, without results, returning at 11:30. At 11:20 the next day, 3-A-301 with Lieutenant Sylvester and 3-A-302 with Lieutenant Lecour left on a similar mission over Punta Federal, although the bad weather over the objective made the mission impossible and the planes returned. After this flight, the four planes were out of service due to different failures, so the mechanics worked constantly until the planes were operational again on 7 June, conducting tactical training flights with Lieutenant Médici in 3-A-301 and Ensign Médici in 3-A-305.

On 8 June, Lieutenant Oliveira (3-A-301) and Lieutenant Olmedo (3-A-305) took off from Río Grande to attack Broken Island, where it was believed that British helicopters were operating. They dropped their five Mk 82 bombs on a building and returned.

On 9 June, Lieutenant Rótolo (3-A-301) and Ensign Medicci (3-A-302) were launched from Río Grande to attack a landing ship stranded in Bahía Fitzroy. After the refuelling and when they were only 19 minutes from the target, the Beechcraft B-200 serial 4-G-44 acting as a relay cancelled the mission due to the presence of three Sea Harriers in the vicinity of the target.

The following day a local training flight was made with 3-A-302 by Lieutenant Benítez and a test flight with 3-A-306, repaired after Zubizarreta's ejection on the ground. This flight was carried out by Lieutenant Sylvester.

Finally, on 12 June, the squadron fulfilled its last mission, Lieutenant Rótolo in 3-A-301 and Lieutenant Medicci in 3-A-302 taking odd to attack artillery pieces north of North Basin. They refuelled from a KC-130 and in the vicinity of their target they encountered two Sea Harriers, forcing them to eject their external loads and return to the mainland, landing in Río Grande.

The 3rd Fighter and Attack Squadron completed thirty-nine operational sorties, in which three aircraft (3-A-307, 312 and 314) and two pilots were lost, thirty-five Mk 82 bombs were dropped, thirty on naval targets and five on land, and 662 20mm rounds fired.

During the war, the Skyhawks received a camouflage paint scheme, in brown and green, that was not the same on all planes. At least 3-A-301, 302, 304, 305 and 306 aircraft received this scheme, while 3-A-308 and 309 were not operational during the war.

A-4Qs after the war with the new grey paint scheme already applied.

This camouflage scheme, as seen on 3-A-304, was applied at Río Grande Naval Air Station after the heavy losses of 21 May 1982.

3-A-304 with the typical gull grey scheme just before the war.

3-A-309 refuelling from an Air Force KC-130H. (*FAA*)

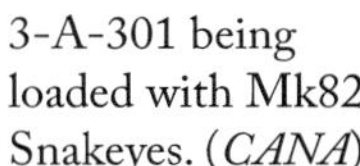

3-A-301 being loaded with Mk82 Snakeyes. (*CANA*)

A pair of A-4Qs aboard the carrier 25 de Mayo. (*CANA*)

Chapter 5

Argentine Air Force Skyhawks in Combat

In 1966 twenty-five refurbished A-4Bs, serialled C-201 to C-225, were acquired from US Navy surplus stocks, followed four years later by a second batch of the same number, C-226 to C-250, equipping Grupo 5 de Caza 'Halcones' ('Hawks') of V Brigada Aérea at Villa Reynolds, San Luis. These aircraft received the A-4P designation for export, although it was rarely used. During the years the Bravos received a few upgrades in Argentina, with an Omega navigation system to about a third of the fleet. In 1976, a third batch was acquired, this time of the A-4C variant, C-301 to C-325, which entered service with Grupo 4 de Caza, IV Brigada Aérea at El Plumerillo air base, Mendoza.

On the eve of the Falklands War, about thirty-six A-4Bs and sixteen A-4Cs were on the FAA active inventory list, although not all were operational. On 14 April and 1 May 1982, Grupo 5 deployed to Río Gallegos air base in the southern Santa Cruz province, activating the temporary I and II Escuadrones de Ataque, each with a strength of eleven A-4Bs. Meanwhile Grupo 4 deployed nine A-4Cs to San Julian air base in the same province, forming the Escuadrón de Ataque A-4C, and these units became part of the recently activated Fuerza Aérea del Sur (Southern Air Force) command. Attrition replacements or aircraft in need of overhauls were flown from/to their respective peacetime bases, where also remained a nucleus of pilots, usually the less experienced ones. Curiously enough the less well equipped A-4Bs were the most successful anti-ship strike aircraft in the Argentine inventory, much more than the Super Étendard/Exocet duet, and among their 'kills' were the ships HMS *Ardent*, *Antelope* and *Coventry*, and the RFAs *Sir Tristram* and *Sir Galahad*, plus many others damaged, but the price paid was very high in aircraft and pilots. The A-4Bs performed 133 operational missions, engaging in combat in 86 of them, losing ten aircraft and nine pilots; the A-4Cs recorded 86 operational missions, engaging in combat in 41, losing nine aircraft and eight pilots.

Eighteen months after the war, the diminishing FAA Skyhawk assets were consolidated in Grupo 5 de Caza, when Grupo 4 transferred its seven surviving A-4Cs on 15 December 1983, and in turn reequipped with ex-IDFAF Mirage IIICJs and BJs. Limited upgrades were undertaken during those years, mainly in the Nav/Attack system, providing capabilities to carry a wider variety of bombs, as well as Shafrir or Magic IR-guided AAMs. Finally after 29 years of operational service, the surviving airworthy A-4Bs and Cs (twelve of the former and four of the later) were phased out of service late in 1995, and Grupo 5 de Caza started to reequip in late 1996 with the first of thirty-six upgraded ex-USMC A-4M Skyhawk IIs; thus this very capable fighter-bomber unit, the 'Hawks', will continue its love affair with the little 'Scooter' well into the twenty-first century.

Capitán Pablo Marcos Carballo of Grupo 5 de Caza of the FAA was an experienced attack pilot with over 1,800 hours in the Skyhawk and a flight leader during the Falklands conflict. A few years later, as a Major, he led a Mirage squadron within Grupo 6 de Caza at Tandil.

Carballo first heard of the Argentine landings near Port Stanley in the early hours of 2 April 1982, while at Villa Reynolds, home of Grupo 5 de Caza, and he gives his first-hand account of some of the events he experienced up to 14 June 1982.

The atmosphere in my squadron was of comradeship, confidence and tension. We clearly understood the importance of the events, and were happy to become witnesses of them, although we clearly saw their implications and that the immediate future held unknown dangers for us all.

Most of Grupo 5 went to Río Gallegos on 14 April 1982, and after establishing at this Patagonian air base, we had to become accustomed to the environment. All of us made orientation flights over the Falklands. On 1 May we flew the first combat mission, which proved to be unsuccessful. Fortunately we didn't suffer losses. From then on we flew anti-shipping sorties with some success – damage to HMS *Glasgow* – and sad losses, four A-4Bs on that day with no survivors among the unfortunate pilots. This was a hammer blow to all of us, four comrades which hours before were living among us.

During the conflict, I had logged a total of 19.55 combat hours over the islands, not counting training, armament practice, surveillance missions, etc, which I flew during those two months. On the combat missions, I reached the target on seven occasions and was hit eight times by the British anti-aircraft defences as follows:

23 May – Surface-to-air missile (SAM) exploded below my Skyhawk, turning it upside down, damaging the rear end of the left drop tank.

25 May – A splinter pierced the left wing.

27 May – My Skyhawk sustained six hits; the first entered through the nose, impacted the left intake, pierced the navigation system, cutting cables, and exited on the right side leaving a hole the size of a soccer ball. The second, which came to chest height, dented a thick metal plate, another broke a rubber conduit, another pierced a drop tank and the last one went right through the tail pipe.

Curiously, on 21 May, during my first attack against a frigate, and due to the desperation with which I pushed the throttle trying to get more speed out of my aircraft, twice I felt it slow down considerably. With my knuckles, and without noticing it I had lowered the landing gear, which speaks volumes for the Skyhawk's strength. I carried a single 1,000lb bomb which I dropped on HMS *Ardent*, my solo attack observed by Alferez Egurza and Private Coronel, two members of the air observers net (ROA) established in the islands.

As a flight leader, I had three pilots almost permanently assigned, with the tactical call-sign Cruz, and usually flew in the following order:

Leader: self
No. 2: Teniente Rinke
No. 3: (section leader) Primer Teniente Cachón
No. 4: Alferez Carmona

My flight was responsible for the attacks on the transports *Sir Tristram* and *Sir Galahad* on 8 June, although I had to abort due to a serious technical malfunction. On that day when I got to my aircraft at the dispersal it had such a serious oxygen leak that I could hear the whistle from outside. Sargento Gamar, the crew chief, advised that I should not fly in these conditions as it could be a one-way ticket. Anyway I flew and later I had more trouble with the fuel system during the air-to-air refuelling stage and had to return home at low level due to lack of oxygen.

After the war a British officer told one of our officers (a POW after the 14 June surrender) that during our attacks on 25 May on HMS *Coventry* and HMS *Broadsword*, one of the ship's Seawolf missile fire-control computers was activated when I attacked with Teniente Rinke. Due to several causes, the FCS started to vacillate, then broke lock and went off, fortunately for us!

After we dropped our bombs on *Broadsword*, when one of mine hit her stern without exploding, but neatly carrying off the nose of the Lynx helicopter, the frigate stopped, the FCS again got a lock, this time on Primer Teniente Velasco and Alferez Barrionuevo. Just as the missiles were to be fired, the destroyer *Coventry* moved between the Skyhawks and the frigate, thus Velasco's bombs hit the Type 42 destroyer dead centre, sinking her in about 20 minutes.

The atmosphere at Río Gallegos was extraordinary, our faith and morale was higher than the fear of sudden death, as we clearly knew what we were fighting for.

Now I would like to describe in detail one of the combat missions I flew. This took place on 27 May, the fragmentary order stated that we would attack British troop concentrations near San Carlos, which were thought to be advancing towards Darwin as night fell. We knew the importance of this mission: it was a way to cooperate with our troops.

At this stage of the conflict with several missions accomplished, we had two feelings, one was fear, as we knew what we could find, and the other was a strange feeling of joy before the danger which heightened all the senses, making one feel in some ways invincible. Also, a deep respect was felt for the enemy, especially one as courageous and professional as the British.

After preparing the navigation and the Omega system had warmed up, we cranked up our engines, taxied out of the dispersals, and gave the thumbs-up signal to the crew chief and the groundcrew which waved an Argentine flag at the side of the runway. We took-off and almost immediately, my Omega went unserviceable, so I let

Teniente Rinke take the lead. We rendezvoused with the KC-130H tanker exactly on time and continued to our IP, on south-west West Falkland/Gran Malvina. Once there, he asked: 'Sir, will you take the lead again?' I replied in the affirmative because at that time, and with several missions under my belt, I knew the islands quite well.

Seven minutes later we were over Grantham Sound/Bahía Ruiz Puente. Two minutes behind us was another section formed by Primer Teniente Velasco and Alférez Osses. Two abandoned orange dinghies on the beach caught my attention, as I flew over the hills I had in front and went into San Carlos.

Then it was like a 'holiday in Montecarlo'. It was late in the afternoon, the frigates were covering big transport vessels, about half a dozen helicopters were carrying slung loads to the beach, and everywhere there was activity. In front of us was the assigned target, San Carlos Settlement. As if somebody pushed a button, the afternoon sky was instantly covered with yellow-orange dots chasing each other. Just in front of us was a thick wall of AA fire.

From the hill, projectiles came towards me and when it seemed they were about to hit, they passed on either side of my aircraft as if there was some kind of protective shield. The SAMs came up in pairs. Rinke shouted: 'What we do?', and I replied, 'Go on Rinke!'. My immediate worry was to see the target and to fly as low as possible. Now the frigates also started to shoot as us. We climbed to 250ft, which was the height for dropping the bombs, and when my pipper was on the pier, I pressed the bomb button, dropping them in sequence. Rinke told me later that the four bombs got a good separation hanging from their parachutes. With the peripheral vision I saw tracers passing closer than the distance from the wingtips to me, and as related previously, six of them hit my Skyhawk.

Coming after us, Velasco and Osses made their runs on the refrigerator plant (we did not know it was then being used as a hospital). Osses took a hit on his drop tanks, while Velasco was riddled and his Skyhawk caught fire in the wing root below the oxygen bottles. I shouted at him to eject while he was flying over a rivulet and dodging the snowcapped hills. Finally he bailed out over West Falkland/Gran Malvina and after some adventurous journeys was recovered by our forces.

I then began to worry about my aircraft. Absolutely nothing worked. The radio was erratic, and with hand signals I indicated to Rinke to take the lead. While my mind worked on the possibilities of 'crossing the pond' in this condition, I formatted in Rinke's wing, almost touching the weaves. Suddenly I saw two aircraft at two o'clock and coming towards us, I thought they were Harriers. I told Rinke but the radio did not work. In desperation I pushed the throttle overhauling him, alternately warping the wings and pushing the throttle to the firewall. He followed me!

Then a thought hit me. Should I jettison the drop tanks to lessen the drag? They were scarce items, so I decided against it. Several minutes later, I indicated by hand signals to Rinke to take the lead again. We started to climb, getting into thick clouds, breaking out of them at 30,000ft, as the sun sank into the horizon and it started to get dark. I knew that I was completely in Rinke's hands, and if I lost him, I should have to eject as most of the instruments did not work.

After a while he made hand signals to reduce the throttle setting to begin our descent, but he did not turn on the navigation lights. Again we entered the clouds, it was hard to maintain position, continually extending and retracting the speed brakes. When he seemed to look at me, I made frantic signals for him to add a little power and to turn on the lights, but he continued without hesitation. In my desperation, I started to insult him (he didn't hear me) and every member of his family. He continued as cold as ice.

After some anguishing minutes, we broke through the cloud base and with Río Gallego's illuminated runway within sight, I forgot about good manners, overtook him and went straight in for a landing.

Just after the wheels touched the concrete, the A-4 jumped like a wild horse, veering towards the side of the runway. One of the main wheels had been punctured by AA fire. I only just avoided going off the runway and after stopping, a pick-up van brought the access ladder.

When climbing down, Sargento Salinas shouted: 'Sir, look at your extreme good luck!' I looked at the aircraft's innards through a hole, then Rinke arrived and we hugged each other. I did not know whether to thank him or to strike him. I started to question him, 'Rinke, why didn't you turn on the navigation lights?'

'Sir, you are getting old. It seems as you are flight leader, it has been a long time since you flew in close formation!'

Again I asked, 'Did you see the two Harriers which were on a reciprocal heading and almost intercepted us?'

'They were Pucarás, Sir!!!'

Teniente Rinke was ice cold, he did not smile or cry, did not talk much, unemotional. In fact he was extremely efficient, courageous and with outstanding self-control.

On 11 June, we were ready to depart on a mission and upon raising my head from some maps I found his stare, and noticed that in his azure blue eyes there was a deep pain, as if he were suffering, but nothing left from his mouth, and his hands – contrary to mine – were steady …

Teniente Luis Alberto Cervera. In February 1974, Cervera was admitted to the Escuela de Aviación Militar at Córdoba. after graduating and completing the fighter/attack course at Mendoza, he was posted to Grupo 5 de Caza in October 1979, becoming combat ready ten months later. He remained with this unit until December 1982, becoming section leader and logging 500+ hours in the A-4B; afterwards he got tours in the Mirage and Dagger with Grupos de Caza 8 and 6 respectively.

On 1 May 1982, Grupo 5 de Caza II Escuadrón to which he was attached was deployed to Río Gallegos, and Cervera took part in the following combat missions:

22 May – Attack against British shipping in San Carlos Water, had to turn back due to technical malfunction during air-to-air refuelling, as he did not have enough fuel to complete the mission.

24 May – Attack against British shipping in San Carlos Water.

28 May – Armed recce over Falkland Sound from north to south and vice versa, without encountering any naval targets.

5 June – Spare pilot for an attack formation, as scheduled returned home when within sight of the islands.

13 June – Attack against the probable site of the British ground forces HQ near Mount Two Sisters.

In the following section, Cervera narrates two of these sorties:

On 24 May two flights were at readiness at Río Gallegos, the first, call-sign 'Nene' was formed by the following pilots:

– Leader: Vicecomodoro (Lieutenant Colonel) Mariel
– No 2: Teniente (Lieutenant) Roca
– No 3: Primer Teniente (1st Lieutenant) Sánchez

The other flight was 'Chispa' with the following:

– Leader: Primer Teniente Berrier
– No. 2: Alferez Moroni
– No. 3: Self

During that morning all of us, the pilots of II Escuadrón of Grupo 5 de Caza under the command of Vicecomodoro Dubourg, were called to the pilots' room for an extensive briefing concerning the tactics to be used during the next mission. After some discussion, the fragmentary order for the mission to be accomplished by the flights arrived.

From then on everything changed, commotion was total, the pilots which remained helped as much as they could, we already were suited with the anti-exposure suit and the anti-G suit, we only had to put on the survival vest to be ready. We planned the navigation in accordance with the references provided by the FAS (Fuerza Aérea del Sur – Southern Air Force) staff.

After everything was ready, we launched from Río Gallegos heading to the ARCP (Air Refuelling Control Point) in absolute radio silence and where a KC-130H was waiting for us. We soon had a visual on the big Hercules orbiting on the briefed map coordinates, all six of us successfully engaged the drogues and with the 'full' showing in the fuel gauges, disengaged. After this uneventful refuelling hop we started our descent to low level while we 'hotted-up' our armament panel. It was while doing this function when I saw the flight leader's bomb – we each carried a Mk 17 1,000lb bomb on the centreline rack – drop, due to a short-circuit in the master armament switch. Without any offensive load, he had to turn back and I occupied his place, while gaining a great wingman, Alferez Moroni, who closed formation until being very near my Skyhawk, providing that kind of support that only an experienced wingie can provide.

After this unfortunate episode, and getting again the attention on the mission to accomplish, we continued to fly about three miles behind Mariel's flight. Flying low over the water was a difficult affair as we had the sun in our front and its reflection on the water made very hard to see in the forward sector. Due to these troublesome reflections, Mariel made a singular mistake when he said: 'look in front!' We all thought it was a frigate, then started the bomb run, but when closer we found that it was a rock rising from the ocean!

After those nervous instants in which we spent a considerable quantity of adrenalin, we continued with our route as briefed, which basically consisted in overflying East Falkland/Isla Soledad, ingressing from the south-west, then arrive over San Carlos Water roughly in an east-west heading, with the sun on our backs, thus making difficult for the AA defences to aim.

After several changes of heading – we got somewhat confused due to the many coves and outlets which dot the shores of the island – we cleared up and set the opportune course.

In absolute radio silence, only broken by the jet engine humming, continually checking the navigation and engine instruments, we continued to route to the target, then I saw Vicecomodoro Mariel pulling up to overfly a small mountain and when he was over the peak I heard in the headset a laconic: 'There they are.'

Instinctively all of us pushed the throttles to the firewall, getting still lower over the rocky terrain, looking for the best ingress place to San Carlos.

I flew over the last hills and then, as in a giant theatre, San Carlos Water just appeared before my eyes, and the show was terrific! Perhaps this these thought through this personal account may seem to happen in hours, but in fact they only lasted seconds.

There were ten to twelve ships on the calm waters, all forming the base for a cone of red tracers. The thought that nobody would leave alive from this hell flashed through my mind. After passing over the hill tops which surrounded the bay, I came down, literally scrapping them and applying some negative Gs, uncomfortable but necessary to perform such terrain masking manoeuvre. While doing this I lost sight of the preceding Skyhawks, then I reached the water and tried to fly as low as I dared. I was going at some 500 knots, and my big dilemma was to choose a ship as a target for my bombs. Soon I saw what seemed an amphibious landing ship big enough and against it I went. I put all my attention on the target which despite being relatively close, it seemed that I never arrived as the AA fire was getting thicker by the moment and the tracers were passing very near and producing big splashes on the water, augmenting my anxiety for reaching the target.

While at some 5ft over the water and 100m from the ship, two A-4Bs crossed in front of me launching their bombs which hit the water a few metres away of 'my' ship's hull.

From the height I was flying, the ship seemed very tall and as I was very close it seemed that I would collide against it, but then I decided it was time to pull back the control stick against my stomach, while at the same time I depressed the bomb release button. I felt how the centreline pylon pyrotechnic charge ejected the bomb. Relieved of 1,000lb of weight, the Skyhawk lurched upwards, I passed over the helicopter deck almost scrapping the rails. Over the ship I made a 90-degree angle of bank and tightened the turn as much as possible; when I was 90 degrees off the previous heading, I brought back the A-4 to level flight, and putting negative Gs I descended to sea level. It was then that I saw pass by my right side two 'things' flying faster than I and leaving small plumes of smoke, both blew up against the hillside to which I was flying near. I assumed they were missiles. When I reached to the hills which I had to overfly to exit from the 'Death Alley', I heard my wingman say in a panic: 'I'm hit! They've got me'. I ordered radio silence, instructing that if he decided to eject, to report over which place in order to alert the rescue forces.

I was relieved after leaving San Carlos Water, although we still had Falkland Sound and West Falkland/Gran Malvina to cross, where the risk of being shot down was still high. After leaving behind our aircraft the last traces of land and over open ocean, I overtook Vicecomodoro Mariel's A-4B, grinned at him and left him behind. With the remaining fuel, I set on the pre-established climb profile to a better cruise height, levelling at 25,000ft on a direct heading to Río Gallegos. With some 200 miles to go before arriving home, Mariel checked in with his flight. The only reply came from Teniente Roca, who said that Primer Teniente Sánchez was with him, and during the mission the later reported trouble with the radio.

Then I felt some anguish when I had to make the radio check with the uncertainty that Moroni would reply. These thoughts lasted for about 20 miles, and at some 180nm from Río Gallegos, I called, receiving the reply: "Great TUCU we return home all and in one piece!' [TUCU is Cervera's nickname and is an abbreviation of his native city, Tucuman – Author.]

We landed at Río Gallegos and there, waiting for us and with happy expressions on their faces were the groundcrews. These men were worth of our highest esteem: they performed a great job 24 hours a day, mostly in the open (not a very nice proposition in this part of the country), to get our aircraft ready for the next mission. Once all of us climbed down and met on the dispersal, we hugged each other with the feeling of happiness of being again together and in one piece ... Río Gallegos, 28 May 1982. The morning hours went slowly, chatting and sipping Mate [an Argentine beverage similar to tea], trying to unload the high tension which accumulated among us. Everyone tried to prepare their flying kit as well as possible, adding candies and cigarettes to the survival kit, the basic idea was to be as comfortable as one could if one had to eject, which nobody wished, but as things were going, it was a distinct possibility.

The weather over the islands was doubtful and if the briefed strike had to be launched, I did not have very clear what could happen. Anyway two flights were at readiness, and these were their members:

1 – Capitán Varela	1 – Vicecom. Dubourg
2 – Alferez Moroni	2 – Alferez Vázquez
3 – Teniente Roca	3 – Teniente Mayor

I acted as spare in case any of them aborted.

Sometime after noon, the low cloud base started to break up and the possibilities of launching became higher. All the assigned pilots were already suited-up with their flying kits, when the fragmentary order arrived from FAS HQ announcing the targets for both alert flights: two frigates seen near Darwin isthmus.

After the briefing we went towards our assigned Skyhawks. As said before, I was spare, ready to occupy the place of any of the six, if any of them had to abort. Consequently the possibilities of taking part on this mission were remote, but not impossible. All seven of us started up the J65s on dispersal and both flights taxied to the runway's threshold, while I remained at dispersal. From there, I saw how the flight led by Captain Varela took-off, while Teniente Mayor, No. 3 of Vicecomodoro Dubourg's flight had a locked wheel, veering off the taxiway and the Skyhawk bogged down in soft ground. I was ordered to take his place in the formation.

I made a fast taxi to the runway, trying to make the pre-take-off checks as fast as possible, as the five A-4s were already in the air. After taking-off and climbing to 20,000ft I established the course to the KC-130H tanker, expecting to arrive on time and join up with the other Skyhawks. This lonely navigation over the unforgiving ocean was worrisome, if something happened to me, nobody would ever would find a trace. I was nearing the AARCP, and started to search for the tanker and the 'little chicks'; my anxiety was such that in every place I could see dots. I continued for a few more minutes with the same speed and height, and then I saw the A-4s milling around the KC-130, when I was closer, I distinguished which drogue was free, so towards it I went. Arriving near the basket I retarded the throttle to idle and deployed the speed brakes in order to slow down and do not overtake, engaging at the first try. As this operation was performed in absolute radio silence, nobody had noticed my integration into the formation, so when I had the tanks full and withdrew from the Hercules, my dilemma was into which of them I should formate, as I did not know who was who, so I waited for the five to establish route formation and then I identified Capitán Varela's A-4B as the 'dapple gray horse', it was C-222 and was called as such because it just had come from an overhaul and been sent to Río

Gallegos as a replacement without receiving the typical camouflage coat. Then I identified the respective flight leaders.

I formatted on Vicecomodoro Doubourg's wing, but he did not know what was going on: he had arrived to the AARCP with a wingman and after topping-up found that he had two! While flying close to the leader at low level over the frosty South Atlantic Ocean, I was checking the instrument panel, when I heard – even with the helmet – the powerful staccato of guns. Surprised because I did not know where they came from, I looked up and saw flashes projecting from the cannon muzzles and a thin trail of smoke from the lead's Skyhawk. He was test firing the guns to check if they worked correctly, without thinking that under radio silence this could cause a heart attack for his wingman. After we landed we laughed at him a long time for such a thing, which 'rabbit' Dubourg fully corresponded to this joke with his fine sense of humour.

Arriving to the islands, the cloud cover was very low, rain squalls and clouds without any intermediate area. Anyway we ingressed without knowing what to expect, but as we flew near West Falkland Island, the cloud base started to rise, settling at about 20–30m above the ocean!. Now we could identify the rocks close to the shore. Once we crossed Falkland Sound and were over East Island, turned left establishing a northern course heading for Grantham Sound. We overflew a hilly area which reduced the free space between the cloud base and the ground, almost reducing visibility to zero, so we had no alternative but to make a left turn and continued flying to the target, but now over the Sound.

It was a big disappointment after such a risky low-level navigation, to arrive over Grantham Sound and find nothing. We were not resigned to return to base without finding a target. At this time, things went a little berserk, as Capitán Varela and his flight continued up to the northern mouth of Falkland Sound, while Vicecomodoro Dubourg choose to perform a 180-degree turn over the Sound, adjacent to San Carlos Water. At that moment the cloud base was at roughly 20m above the water, and to both sides of the sun the shore rose in almost vertical walls quite impressive, it was like making this manoeuvre inside a shoe box. At half turn, as I was flying as number three and in order not to lose them from sight, I decided to tighten the turn in order to reduce the radius of the half circle, consequently I would shorten my separation, but without losing into the clouds the A-4 flown by Alferez Vázquez. But sometimes things do not develop as one wishes, and he almost overstressed his aircraft to avoid what seemed a mid-air collision, I crossed to the other side, going through the reduced space between him and the water. This was the only possible way of doing this change of position, as doing it over Vázquez was out of the question because of the low clouds, and the risk that I should lose from sight everything in such a narrow place. Fortunately the manoeuvre went well, but it is still engraved in my mind as a colour picture, the oil-stained belly of Vázquez's Skyhawk. After all three of us were on a rough southern heading, we could relax a little, although we tried to find a secondary target without any luck, and much to our sorrow, the diminishing fuel level forced us to return to our base with the bomb loads still attached. Thanks to God everybody returned, and if the terrible weather complicated and frustrated our mission, the same was for the British defences which never had us within sight. That night our squadron CO bought us several rounds of whisky in the mess … San Julian air base, 13 June 1982 – I will start the account of the day's events some journeys previously. On 8 June which we nicknamed the 'Task Force's Blackest Day' when at Fitzroy we attacked and mortally damaged the LSTs *Sir Galahad* and *Sir Tristram*, but also, we had to face the terrible rigour and cruelty of any war, losing three members of a flight from my squadron; the only survivor was Primer Teniente Sánchez. During the following day (9 June) we had to redeploy both A-4B squadrons to San Julian to join-up with the A-4C squadron already operating from there, while in turn the Dagger squadron went to Río Gallegos. I made this particular flight with Capitán Varela, Primer Teniente Sánchez and myself forming a flight. In order to practice low level flying we cut across the ocean, going 25 miles out into it, as a pilot needs a lot of practice to train his eyes to this form of flying, and as any mistake could mean finishing in a wet grave. While flying in such a way with the formation in combat spread, my heart started to beat faster for what my eyes had seen: slowly but progressively the EGT was descending, under this circumstance, I took advantage of the speed – 480 knots – climbing as hard as possible while turning towards the mainland, so I could be over firm ground if the engine stopped. When I passed over the beach the EGT had reached zero degrees centigrade, but the old J65 continued to run smoothly, and after landing at San Julian we found the cause of such anxious moments, a thermocouple malfunction, thanks to God.

We had to adapt quickly to the new environment in San Julian air base, sleeping quarters, mess, etc. but for us the change was important, as at Río Gallegos we felt at home, receiving the attention of the civilian community from the nearby city, and although the same happened at San Julian, it was different. A few hours after arriving everybody had quarters, either within the base or in hotels at San Julian city.

Despite the high losses suffered, the moral was high at Grupo 5 de Caza, as an example, from seventeen pilots posted to our squadron at the start of the hostilities, we had lost nine, but the fighting spirit continued to be as high as the first day, and we had received new replacement pilots just off operational conversion, plus transfers from the other component squadron of Grupo 5. [II Escuadrón was hard hit by luck as it suffered 90 per cent of Grupo 5's losses in aircraft and pilots. I Escuadrón only lost one A-4B, and its pilot survived – Author.]

In such conditions the date of 13 June arrived, with two flights at readiness:

'Nene'	'Chispa'
1 – Capitán Zelaya	1 – Capitán Varela
2 – Teniente Gerardi	2 – Teniente Roca
3 – Teniente Cervera	3 – Teniente Mayor
4 – Alferez Dellepiane	4 – Alferez Moroni

While waiting at the pilots' room, we were informed that we should make the first and only close-air-support (CAS) mission for Grupo 5 de Caza during the entire war. We had to attack a British troop concentration and HQ area near Mount Two Sisters. Once all details for this mission were coordinated, each one of us went to his Skyhawk. Mine was C-212, clearly remembering its serial for a reason that I would reveal later during the mission.

I did the external walkaround, while the ground crews and armourers wished us good luck. My flight was launched first, except Alferez Dellepiane, which had to take the spare aircraft due to a technical malfunction during engine start-up, so he took off slightly later and with Capitán Varela's flight. During the leg to the AARCP, my thoughts were for my family, as it was the only time during the mission when I could distract my attention.

With absolute radio silence, we proceeded to refuel from the KC-130H, and then I saw, that our flight leader, Capitán Zelaya, without topping up his tanks, disengaged violently from the basket and started a steep descent. Breaking radio silence I asked him if he had any trouble; his reply confirmed my fears, his engine temperature gauge was on the red due to fuel ingestion by the compressor caused by a leak in the refuelling system. On these conditions he could not continue the mission having to return to base, so I took the lead from him.

At this moment, Capitán Varela, 'Chispa' flight leader, requested me that he become the leader of the mission due to his higher experience, so he led the attack, while I positioned some 12/15 seconds behind his flight, the best distance to avoid the blast from their bombs. After the refuelling operation we started to descend, keeping visual contact with the 'Chispas' and checking in the Omega navigation system that we were in the correct route.

The descent was difficult due to several cloud layers present in the area. When the 'Chispas' went through them I lost the Skyhawks from sight. Transitioning to IFR conditions we went through the mass of clouds following the heading and descent rate, when we emerged from them, I found that the leading flight was ahead of and below us. We had gone through five cloud layers. Once flying low over the water, it was very easy to keep the 'Chispas' within visual contact, as they flew so low that the exhaust from their jet pipes produced a remarkable trail on the ocean's surface, as if they were offshore boats! It was really impressive to see them so low. We arrived to the north-west of West Falkland/Gran Malvina and now flying over ground, we heard our radar controller at Port Stanley calling: 'Is anybody flying?' to which both flight leaders replied, giving course and details about the target we intended to attack. It was then when the controller gave us valuable information concerning the location of Sea Harrier CAPs – one flying over Fitzroy, and the other two flying over the northern and southern ends of Falkland Sound, so we found out that we were cornered in our possible escape routes after the attack.

Studying the situation I told Capitán Varela, that perhaps it could be a good idea to return using the same route that we were following now, knowing that his was not covered by the deadly Sea Harriers, altogether there was the risk of making a 180-degree turn under the enemy's noses, but it was less dangerous than meeting a CAP. He replied affirmatively. We were very near the target, and it was harder to follow the 'Chispas', as heading changes were quite frequent, while the rolling terrain caused to lose them from sight sometimes. With my attention fully fixed on not losing them, I was quite surprised when I heard Capitán Varela say to his flight: 'Bombs away, go!', then I saw the explosions of the twelve bombs. Feeling bad for my wingmen who perhaps could not follow me, I made a hard turn towards the area were the bombs had exploded as the target was there. During the attack run, I started to fire the Colt Mk 12 cannon as a defensive measure to keep heads down. Near the target I could not see very well due to the smoke and dirt produced by the preceding flight bombs and while overflying it I saw four or five helicopters destroyed, while people ran in every direction. I did not drop the bombs as I thought that I could find as intact target [only light damage was caused by the bombs of 'Chispa' flight – Author]. After getting clear of the smoke and confusion, I saw more helicopters and troops running, there we dropped our bombs. During the egress I met a Sea King helicopter flying perpendicular to me from right to left. As I had the sight collimated for 260 mils – for low-level bombing – I started to shoot my guns by eyesight my, seeing the streak of tracers converging into the big helicopter. I came dangerously close to the Sea King, seeing clearly the light blue helmets of the pilots, then with ammo spent, I pulled up and passed over it as in slow motion. [This was a Sea King HC.4 of No 846 Sqn, and the only damage was a hole in a rotor blade caused by a 20mm round; a precautionary landing was made and after changing the blade, the helicopter was again in the air – Author]. After this manoeuvre and when I had levelled my Skyhawk, I heard Alferez Dellepiane desperate call: 'TUCU break right!, break right!'. I did immediately, putting 90 degrees of bank trying to do the turn as tight as possible, while at the same time I jettisoned all external stores, drop tanks and multiple ejector racks. Simultaneously, I saw a pair of missiles with a bright flame on their rear end pass very close to my left side, fast as hell. While in the panic turn, and after releasing the stores, the A-4 skidded down, and only a few feet separated the hard ground from my right wingtip. In such a situation I had no alternative but to put wings level, relaxing the turn and gain some height to make a safer getaway.

From then I did not see any more of my wingman during the rest of the flight and I felt uneasy about it as during the return leg we needed each other for mutual support. While continuing with the escape, I did not cease swivelling my head from side to side to clear my rear, then to my surprise I noticed over the ground the shadow of an aircraft to the right and rear. I took it as a Sea Harrier and started to jink and make evasive manoeuvres but each time that I looked to the right the shadow continued with its implacable pursuit. My worry dissipated later when after several more manoeuvres, I found it was the shadow of my own aircraft!

Certainly and without any excuse it was quite embarrassing, but in the high stress level in which I was at the moment, it was perhaps a logical reaction. All the clothing I had under the anti-exposure suit was wet from perspiration, so I made an effort to get the adrenaline flowing to its normal level. I went over the beach through the north-east of East Falkland, putting the trusty Skyhawk very low over the ocean, while I continued to scan the rear hemisphere for any Sea Harrier CAP.

When I became convinced that I was alone, I tried to pay more attention to the navigation and then I noticed that I only had 2,000lbs of fuel remaining, when the minimum for a safe base return was 1,900lbs. Just after starting the climb to optimum cruise height, I saw at right angles to my flight path a frigate, it was as if the warship had risen up from under the sea as I should had seen it before. Without losing it from view, I made an easy left turn until being parallel, trying to observe any possible missile launch. Incredibly it did not. When I thought that the separation was sufficient, I started to climb again and at 10,000ft I entered clouds, leaving them above 30,000ft, continuing the climb until I reached 45,000ft and once level I settled the throttle at Bingo Power Setting, to save fuel as I thought I would not reach San Julian. I had the hope of aerial refuelling, but this proved vain, as Alferez Dellepiane had been hit in one of the wing tanks, so he had to go 'towed' by the KC-130H up to the airfield, so I elected to leave both drogues to him. In fact he engaged one of the baskets when the fuel gauge was reading zero.

At about 110 miles from San Julian flying at 45,000ft and with 300lbs of fuel remaining, I put the throttle to ide and started a gentle descent, trying to get the best glide angle, passing through three cloud layers until I saw the runway. Then I asked the tower for an emergency straight approach. At about ten miles I saw in front of me another A-4B also on finals, asking his pilot how much fuel he had, Moroni replied about 1,000lbs, and on learning of my difficulties he cleared the area, performing a 360-degree turn to land after me. Thus I touched down safely with 100lbs of fuel remaining in the tanks. I taxied to the dispersal and turned off the engine. I stayed in the cockpit, very nervous, thinking what had happened to my wingman, Alferez Dellepiane. While waiting for him I noticed that several ground crews had gathered around my Skyhawk talking among themselves. I asked myself what was the curiosity with C-212. Then appeared the KC-130H Hercules with Dellepiane in two, until short final where he disengaged and landed; when the wheels touched the runway, a cloud of sprayed fuel covered the aircraft. Dellepiane stopped the Skyhawk on the runway and quickly vacated it just in case something started a fire.

Now I was much more tranquil thanks to the mission's happy end, climbing down the cockpit I could observe four holes on the vertical fin, unbelievably they went through it without touching the hydraulic lines. I met the pilots of the two flights, we were very, very happy to be alive, and although we didn't know at the time, ours was the last Grupo 5 combat mission of the war …

A-4B Slayer

Three of the ten A-4Bs lost by Grupo 5 de Caza were shot down by Fleet Air Arm Sea Harrier FRS.1s, all on the 8 June raids carried out by Argentine Skyhawks against the British beachhead at Pleasant Bay, Flight Lieutenant David Morgan, an RAF exchange pilot flying with 800 Naval Air Squadron aboard HMS *Hermes* claimed two, here is his account:

> On 8 June I was flying Sea Harrier ZA177 with Lieutenant Smith as my wingman when we were sent to fly CAP (Combat Air Patrol) over Port Pleasant where the LSTs *Sir Tristram* and *Sir Galahad* had been attacked and damaged. We arrived there shortly before sunset, and had been on CAP for about 20 minutes when I saw an aircraft running in to attack a small landing craft about eight miles south of us. I dived down from 10,000ft with Lieutenant Smith one mile behind me, but I was not able to get there before the second aircraft scored a hit with one of his bombs. A third aircraft attacked and missed and I saw a fourth aircraft which did not attack and I believe that it may have trying to engage a Sea King helicopter that was in the area. I ended up behind this aircraft at 100ft doing about 650 knots and fired my first missile at about 1,000 yards range. The missile homed perfectly and the target exploded instantly. No ejection was seen. I then locked-up the third man and fired at about 1,800 yards at a height of 50ft. He saw the missile launch and broke right but the warhead blew the back half of the aircraft away from just in front of the tail fin and the fuselage hit the water within seconds. This pilot ejected and his parachute opened just in front of my left wing.
>
> I now engaged the other two aircraft with ADEN guns. My HUD went out at this stage and I fired a short burst from about 1,200 yards with both aircraft in the centre of my windscreen but without any aiming mark. This caused one aircraft to break left and I followed it at about 50ft closing in to 300 yards with both guns firing but without a gunsight, I was unable to hit it. When I ran out of bullets I pulled straight up into a vertical climb and rolled out at about 15,000ft heading for home. Meanwhile Lieutenant Smith had not seen me after I started my dive and was not sure where everyone was but saw my bullets exploding on the sea and saw an aircraft flying through them. It was quite dark at this stage and he could not identify the aircraft until he saw me pull out. He then fired a Sidewinder at the speeding Skyhawk and hit it very low as it approached Hammond Point. There was no ejection. When we landed on *Hermes* we had less two minutes' fuel remaining …

Argentine Air Force Skyhawk Losses – Falklands War

A-4B // Grupo 5 De Caza

C-204 – Shot down on 8 June 1982 by a 800 NAS Sea Harrier flown by Lieutenant Smith over Choiseul Sound, pilot Primer Teniente Bolzán killed.

C-206 – Crashed into the sea off Port Stanley on 12 May 1982 while attacking HMS *Glasgow* and HMS *Brilliant* due to hard evasive actions while avoiding Sea Wolf SAMs, pilot Teniente Nivoli killed.

C-208 – Shot down by a Sea Wolf fired from HMS *Brilliant* off Port Stanley on 12 May 1982, pilot Teniente Ibarlucea killed.

C-215 – Shot down by 40mm Bofors AA fire from HMS *Fearless* after successfully attacking British positions at Ajax Bay on 27 May 1982, pilot Primer Teniente Velasco ejected near Port Howard, West Falkland.

C-226 – Shot down over Choiseul Sound on 8 June 1982 by an 800 NAS Sea Harrier flown by Flight Lieutenant Morgan, pilot Teniente Arrarás killed.

C-228 – Shot down over Choiseul Sound on 8 June 1982 by an 800 NAS Sea Harrier flown by Flight Lieutenant Morgan just after scoring a direct bomb hit on the landing craft 'Foxtrot-4' from HMS *Fearless*, pilot Alferez Vázquez ejected but killed.

C-242 – Shot down by SAM/AA/small-arms fire in San Carlos Water while attacking the frigate HMS *Antelope* on 23 May 1982, pilot Primer Teniente Guadagnini killed.

C-244 – Shot down by Sea Dart SAM from HMS *Coventry* north of Pebble Island on 25 May 1982, pilot Capitán Palaver killed.

C-246 – Shot down by Sea Wolf SAM from HMS *Brilliant* off Port Stanley on 12 May 1982, pilot Primer Teniente Bustos killed.

C-248 – Shot down by (mistaken) Argentine 35mm AA fire over Goose Green on 12 May 1982, pilot Primer Teniente Gavazzi killed.

A-4C // Grupo 4 De Caza

C-301 – Shot down east of the Falklands by Sea Dart SAM from HMS *Exeter* on 30 May 1982, pilot Primer Teniente Vázquez killed.

C-303 – Crashed into the ocean in bad visibility near South Jason Island, north-west of West Falkland on 9 May 1982, pilot Teniente Farias killed.

C-304 – Shot down by Sea Dart SAM from HMS *Coventry* north of Pebble Island on 25 May 1982, pilot Capitán García ejected but died of exposure.

C-305 – Shot down by AA fire, crashing in King George Bay, West Falkland, pilot Teniente Bono killed.

C-309 – Shot down on 21 May 1982 over West Falkland by Sea Harrier of 800 NAS flown by Lieutenant Commander Thomas, pilot Teniente López killed.

C-310 – Shot down east of the Falklands by Sea Dart SAM from HMS *Exeter* on 30 May 1982, pilot Primer Teniente Castillo killed.

C-313 – Crashed into high ground at South Jason Island (north-west of West Falkland) on 9 May 1982, pilot Teniente Casco killed.

C-319 – Shot down over San Carlos Water by AA fire and Rapier SAM on 25 May 1982, pilot Teniente Lucero ejected.

C-325 – Shot down over West Falkland on 21 May 1982 by Sea Harrier of 800 NAS flown by Lieutenant Commander Blissett, pilot Primer Teniente Manzotti killed.

ELMA *Formosa*, attacked by mistake on 1 May 1982.

Armed with three 250kg BR bombs each, these Skyhawks are ready for a mission in the last days of the war.

1st Lieutenant Fausto Gavazzi flies low towards HMS *Glasgow* on 12 May. One of his bombs put the ship out of action, but he was shot down by friendly anti-aircraft artillery at Goose Green when he was returning.

ELMA *Río Carcarañá*.

Ensign Schwind, Ensign 'Toba' Nieto, Captain Carballo and Lieutenant 'Tom' Lucero (from Fighter Group 4). The aircraft is armed with a 454kg AN M65 bomb with Mk 17 tail, known locally as a 'Bombola'.

The apron at San Julián, with four A-4Bs, one Aerocommander 500U, one Hughes 500 and the Chaco Province government Bell 212.

A Skyhawk escapes from British anti-aircraft artillery at San Carlos.

The Skyhawks of Velasco and Barrionuevo are received by the ground crews after sinking the *Coventry*.

C-224 prepared for a mission at Río Gallegos.

A-4B and C ready for a mission.

Captain Pablo Carballo, left, and Lieutenant Carlos Rinke, right, attacking HMS *Broadsword* on 25 May.

Ensign Dellepiane's A-4B returns leaking fuel from its mission on 13 June, when it was hit by anti-aircraft fire.

Captain Palaver flying in C-244 on 1 May 1982, when he was part of the Topo Squadron. On 25 May Palaver would be shot down by a Sea Dart missile from HMS *Coventry*, shortly before the destroyer was sunk by Mariano Velasco's A-4B.

Lieutenant Daniel Gálvez in the C-206 flying away from the KC-130H that refuelled it on its way to the islands on 1 May 1982 when he was part of the Topo Squadron.

Ensign Hugo Gómez in C-225 refuelling in flight on 1 May, en route to the Falklands as part of the Topo Squadron.

1st Lieutenant Luciano Guadagnini refuelling in flight in C-221 on 1 May 1982, when he was flying as part of the Topo Squadron. On 23 May it was shot down by the frigate HMS *Antelope*, although it managed to make a hit with its bomb, which exploded while being defuzed, causing the sinking of the ship.

June 13th 1982, San Julián, day of the last mission of the A-4Bs over the Falklands. Photo Hector Tessio.

The A-4B registration C-250 seen in San Julián on 13 June 1982, one day before the end of the war.

The frigate HMS *Antelope* breaks in two and sinks in San Carlos Bay on the morning of 24 May 1982, after the bomb dropped by First Lieutenant Luciano Guadagnini exploded.

The destroyer HMS *Coventry* is blown to pieces on 25 May 1982 by at least two of the three 250kg Expal bombs dropped by Mariano Velasco.

The *Coventry* capsized and sank in less than half an hour. According to the survivors, it was a nightmare to escape from the ship, without any power, heeled over, with fire and smoke inside. Only five of the life rafts could be used.

RFA *Sir Galahad* in flames after being hit by bombs on 8 June 1982.

A-4B, registration C-212, deployed in San Julián at the end of the war.

This Skyhawk did not participate in the war.

A-4B and C flight line at V Air Brigade in the 1980s after the war.

The A-4B C-212 with an experimental paint scheme tested after the war to reduce the visibility of the aircraft.

Another of the low-visibility paint schemes tested in the 1980s, before it ceased flying in 1985.

A-4B C-222 refuelling in flight during a firing exercise, carrying Mk 12 practice bombs.

An A-4B hooks up the braking cable at the end of the V Air Brigade runway.

130kg bombs are loaded into a Multiple Ejector Rack on an A-4C.

An A-4B, carrying a 125kg bomb made in Argentina, makes a low-level pass. The aircraft has the 30mm guns.

TA-4B C-225 seen in Mendoza, with four 127mm LAU-10 four-tube rocket pods.

A-4B C-231 with an unusual paint scheme, with the ventral part in light blue.

An A-4B during tests of the six-tube 70mm rocket pod manufactured in Argentina by Tensa. These were not eventually adopted by the air force.

An A-4B in the sights of an IAI M5 Finger during a combat exercise of different performance in the 1980s.

An A-4B of the Argentine Air Force and a Super Étendard of the Naval Aviation Command refuelling in flight from a KC-130H.

An A-4C refuelling from an A-4B using the Buddy Pack. This system was used only for training and not in combat.

Two A-4Bs refuelling from a KC-130H Hercules in the early 1980s.

C-209 after crash-landing at Salar del Tolillar, Salta province, on 23 June 1994. Part of the wreckage still remains at the site.

An A-4B refuelling in flight over Patagonia in the early 1990s. The aircraft has 30mm cannon. (*Photo Gustavo D'Antocchia*)

Flight line of seventeen A-4Bs and at least one A-4C (at the end) in 1992, by which time Fighter Group 5 still had thirty aircraft in service between the two Skyhawk models.

Flight line in the V Air Brigade after the war, with some A-4Bs sporting marks of ships damaged or sunk during the war. C-212 was the aircraft used by Mariano Velasco to sink HMS *Coventry*.

C-240 in the 1990s. The aircraft is equipped with an A-4C engine, which was indicated by painting the nose white.

FAS-250 parachute-braked tail-finned bombs, designed locally by the Argentine Air Force Systems Directorate.

When the 20mm guns were not used, the place where the barrels came out was covered with a special fairing. (*Photo Juan Carlos Cicalesi*)

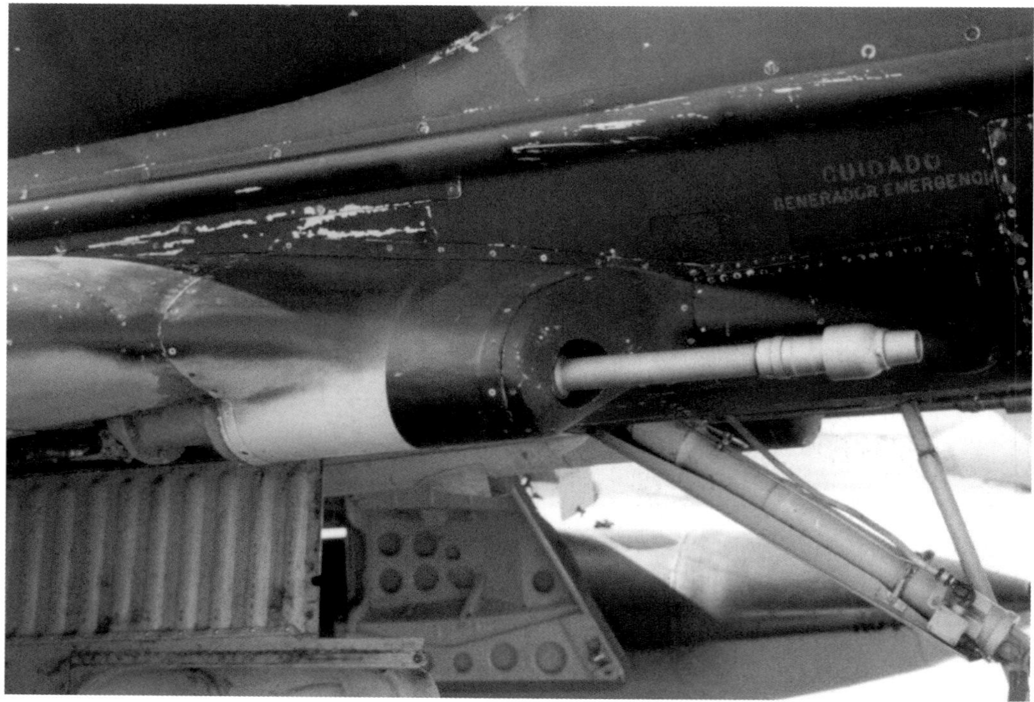

Modification for the installation of two 30mm DEFA553A-4 guns on an A-4B.

An A-4C descends towards its target during an exercise in Neuquén province in 1986. Photo Commodore Raúl H. Paz.

Refuelling an A-4C through the in-flight refuelling probe.

An A-4C preparing for take-off. The shades of brown of its paint scheme were not standardized, so they varied over time and on each aircraft.

An A-4C in flight in the mid-1980s. (*Photo Commodore Raúl H. Paz*)

An A-4B and an A-4C flying in formation with a KC-130H Hercules refuelling aircraft.

An A-4C refuelling in flight, armed with six IMI PG 130 Mk 3 130kg bombs on the belly mount, Condib Mk 70 anti-runway bombs on the inner sub-wing mounts and two Shafrir 2 exercise bombs on the outer mounts.

A-4C armed with six IMI PG 130 Mk 3 130kg bombs on the belly mount, Condib Mk 70 anti-runway bombs on the inner sub-wing mounts and two Shafrir 2 exercise bombs on the outer mounts.

An A-4C in flight with a Matra R-550 Magic test missile during the homologation of these missiles on the aircraft to replace the Shafrir 2.

An A-4C fires an R-550 Magic missile during the homologation tests of the missiles on these aircraft.

An A-4C with an R-550 Magic exercise missile. Due to the limited availability of these missiles, they were no longer used on A-4Cs after type approval and were left for the Mirage IIIEA.

An A-4C during the testing of the Thomsom-Brandt/MATRA BLG-66 Belouga cluster bombs.

Two A-4Cs are refuelled with a R-550 Magic missile. Two A-4Cs refuelling in flight from a KC-130H.

An OA-4AR prepares to attach its refuelling probe to the Buddy Pack carried by an A-4B, in 1997. (*Photo Daniel Berástegui*)

A-4B registration C-225 with badly-deteriorated paintwork in the early 1990s.

C-225 takes off from the V Air Brigade in September 1998. (*Photo Santiago Rivas*)

Flight line of A-4B, A-4C, A-4AR and OA-4AR at the V Air Brigade in September 1998. (*Photo Santiago Rivas*)

A-4C C-314 and A-4B C-225 taking off from the V Air Brigade during a training flight in September 1998. (*Photo Santiago Rivas*)

A-4B C-225 and A-4C C-322 on a pass with everything down in September 1998. (*Photo Santiago Rivas*)

A-4C C-322 taking off from the V Air Brigade in 1998. (*Photo Santiago Rivas*)

A-4B C-225 in a low pass and with gear and hook down, over the V Air Brigade. (*Photo Santiago Rivas*)

C-225 in a low pass in front of the V Air Brigade control tower in 1998. (*Photo Santiago Rivas*)

A-4C C-322 makes a very low pass over the V Air Brigade in its last year of service. With the arrival of the A-4ARs in 1997, the old Skyhawks were relegated to training duties. (*Photo Santiago Rivas*)

A-4B C-214 in its last year of service. In 1999 it was placed as a memorial at the V Air Brigade. (*Photo Santiago Rivas*)

C-322 in its last months of service. It was the last A-4C to fly in Argentina. (*Photo Santiago Rivas*)

Crews and mechanics who participated in the farewell of the A-4B and C of the FAA on 15 March 1999, minutes before taking off for the parade that marked the end of their career. (*Photo Santiago Rivas*)

A-4C C-322 and A-4B C-207 arriving at the National Museum of Aeronautics, at BAM Morón, Buenos Aires, in early April 1999, in what was the last flight of both models in Argentina. (*Photo Fernando Benedetto*)

Chapter 6

Lieutenant Commander Rodolfo Castro Fox. C.O. Tercera Escuadrilla Aeronaval de Caza y Ataque

'On 29 March we embarked on the aircraft carrier *25 de Mayo*, with three A-4Q aircraft and five qualified pilots, with the mission of supporting the operations for the recovery of the Falklands Islands. Only the commanders knew the destination of that sailing and Stella said goodbye to me in the belief that we would be making another routine sea leg.

During the night of 1 April and the early morning of the 2nd, with a portable radio and installed in the control tower of the aircraft carrier, I followed the Port Stanley radio transmission step by step.

I was not surprised by the phlegm of the islander announcer who was communicating with different inhabitants in the vicinity of the city and receiving the accounts of how the advances of the Argentine troops were being detected, with voices barely affected by the events they were experiencing.

They described the movements of combatants, the areas where gunfire was heard and some comments made without any abnormal or emotional overtones. Then the radio was taken over and communiqués were made in Spanish and English for population control.

That morning, I presided over the formation of the Squadron's embarked men, who could not hide their joy at hearing of the successful recovery of the Islands. The support of our aircraft had not been necessary, but it was on that occasion that I conveyed to them my conviction that from that moment on we must work hard because for us the task had only just begun.

On 6 April we landed at Puerto Belgrano and began an extraordinary activity. The pilots recently incorporated to the Squadron, without experience in the A-4, were transferred to their previous operational destinations, as in the case of Lieutenant Guillermo Owen Crippa, who later had an outstanding performance flying the Aermacchi MB-339A, when he attacked individually with 127mm rockets and 30mm cannons the frigate HMS *Argonaut* on 21 May, while performing an armed reconnaissance flight that detected the landing of the British forces in San Carlos.

Lieutenant Commanders Gabriel Alejandro Richmond, Roberto Diego Loubet Jambert and Pablo Miguel Linari were assigned to the same attack squadron. So was Frigate Lieutenant Diego Luis Goñi, who was in the primary stage of his training in the A-4, although in the last days of operation he was reincorporated into the Squadron to collaborate in maintenance flights.

At the same time we incorporated the pilots who had been transferred to other destinations at the end of 1981. Lieutenant Commander Jorge A. Philippi was returning from Río Grande, Navy Lieutenants Benito I. Rótolo and José C. Arca would do so from a more distant place, France, where they were about to begin their flight course in the Super Étendard.

Lieutenant Carlos Oliveira and Lieutenant Alejandro Olmedo would also join the fleet. There were seven aircraft that were out of service due to cracks in the central wing spar; three of them had their wings replaced and were fitted with A-4B wings that had the additional spare cells with modifications for spoilers. Two of the aircraft flew with these cracks during operations and the remaining two remained in the Central Naval Aircraft Workshop during the conflict (3-A-308 and 3-A-309) while the wings were replaced.

The ESCAPAC 1-A1 seat ejector rockets had expired on 30 December 1981, and in order to equip the incorporated aircraft, by order of the Commander of Naval Air Force No. 2, for real operational purposes and for the duration of the conflict, the life of the expired MK-1 Mod 1 seat ejector cartridges was extended. This measure was taken without technical support. During August 1981, after my accident, and due to the late ejection of the ejection seat, an MK-1 rocket booster had been ground tested and this experience had been satisfactory. With my second-in-command, Lieutenant Commander Carlos Zubizarreta, we agreed that for a cartridge that had a service life of 60 months installed, the extension would be within the safety margin taken by the manufacturer for its use.

Although I was not authorized to fly due to the physical after-effects of the accident, I informed my superior that I would do so in order to lead my pilots, as I would not be grounded in the event of combat.

On 9 April I made my first flight after eight months of inactivity. I had some problems in the operation of the plane; among them I could not open or lock the cockpit because of the effort that my injured arm required to operate the lever for that purpose, located on the left, but the mechanics did it from the outside of the plane. Nor could I move the lever to raise the landing gear for the same reason, and I had to take the flight stick in my left hand and cross my right arm to operate the gear control on the left.

Likewise, the switches on the left rear sector were reached by resting my hand on the console and moving my fingers and dragging my arm backwards until I could operate them.

In a week, with a little more than seven hours of flight time, I was ready to go to the aircraft carrier again; I had flown instrumental, night, performed practice bombing and low-level bombing, refuelled in flight with the KC-130 'Hercules' of the Argentine Air Force and made almost thirty PTAP landings.

On 18 April we embarked on the aircraft carrier with twelve pilots and eight aircraft, and after re-qualifying the seven of us who had rejoined, we carried out attack exercises on the ARA destroyers *Hercules* and *Santísima Trinidad*, which were Type 42s – similar to HMS *Sheffield* – guided by the Grumman Trackers that operated from the aircraft carrier.

The tactics of the attacks were based on the doctrine developed during 1978, when experiments had been carried out with the support of the Operational Research Group of the National University of the South, led by retired Naval Aviator Captain Gerardo Sylvester. In order to approach undetected to this type of air defence ships equipped with 965 air-control radars, we had to fly less than 500ft within 100 nautical miles, then less than 100ft within 50 nautical miles and finally fly less than 50ft (15m) within 30nm. In this way we penetrated below their radar emission lobe and prevented the 30nm range Sea Dart surface-to-air missile launches. In the final phase of the attack we would manoeuvre to avoid the point of impact of radar-guided cannon fire, based on the calculation of missile flight and changes in course.

With three aircraft we had to manoeuvre to avoid passing over the target with a time separation of between 5 and 20 seconds. In order to avoid the shrapnel from the explosions of the bombs dropped by the previous planes in the attack, the planned manoeuvre with changes in course took us an interval of more than 20 seconds. At the same time we attacked from different sectors approaching the target to make it difficult for the anti-aircraft guns to aim. The low bombing launch was planned with 300ft of height, so that with two seconds of delay armed with the fuze (the minimum possible of those we used) the bomb would be armed in a fall of 200ft and if it hit a structure, to have the margin of 100ft of height to ensure the explosion.

The time delay of the fuze, set at 25 milliseconds, allowed for penetration and subsequent explosion inside the structure. By releasing up to six 500lb bombs with a multiple launcher, we applied automatic release with an interval of 200 milliseconds between bombs, which at 450 knots of speed, allowed the Snakeye bombs to fall 40m apart and, dropped at 45 degrees to the ship's centreline, the probability of impact of at least one bomb, for the neutralisation of the target, was very high.

We had passed these experiences on to the pilots of the Argentine Air Force, who at that time were at the Espora Naval Air Base. The weapons we had were different, but our main insistence was that they should avoid approaching at high altitude, because from 150nm with 965 radars they would be detected and this would facilitate the interception of the CAPs (Combat Air Patrols with Sea Harrier aircraft equipped with AIM-9L Sidewinder missiles) or the launching of Sea Dart missiles with a range of 30nm and also, the early detection of the attack would enable radar-directed naval anti-aircraft fire, which would therefore be more precise. We also warned the same pilots that a glide bomb strike would be unlikely because of the time it would take to fly the bomb and the manoeuvrability of the ship at 30 knots speed in the open sea.

The American Mk 82 500lb delayed-tail bomb in our arsenal allowed it to be dropped in low-level flight, and to be delayed in its fall with respect to the aircraft by the aerodynamics of increased drag, due to the four large plates that deployed after being dropped. In this way, when they exploded, their effect did not reach the launching aircraft that had gone ahead of them.

To ensure that the bombs fell with the fuze armed after release, we tied the wires that activate the tail and nose fuzes to the aircraft's launcher structure, instead of connecting them to the solenoids provided for this purpose. The latter is the normal procedure, which allows the bomb to be dropped armed, or if necessary – via a switch in the cockpit – without arming the fuze when the solenoid is opened and the wire detached for arming. As these alternatives could fail, we did not use them and thus ensured that the fuzes would always be armed when the bomb was released and ready to initiate the bomb explosion. In an emergency we would drop the bombs over the sea and they would explode there.

During this stage we also carried out air-interception exercises, conducted by the carrier's radars and its escort ships, on Air Force aircraft operating south of Comodoro Rivadavia and simulating attacks on the Fleet.

We landed on 25 April at the Puerto Belgrano Naval Base and over the next couple of days, two aircraft were fitted with VLF Omega navigation equipment to improve navigation conditions over the sea. This had been a constant demand in previous years, but the Navy leadership always found reasons for not doing so, in the same way that our requests to install 30mm cannon on the A-4s to increase the possibility of fire and reliability in use were never heard. We also installed OTPI equipment on two other aircraft, as an experiment, which are sonobuoy receivers used in anti-submarine warfare by Tracker aircraft to track their emissions when they are launched into the sea. Its purpose was to be able to land on a sonobuoy dropped by a Tracker aircraft over the sea, and from there to have a bearing and distance of a target given by the scout aircraft that could not stay in the area, either because of its range or because of enemy threats.

We embarked again on 28 April and on that occasion during the flight to the aircraft carrier I began to feel the symptoms of renal colic, so familiar from having suffered from them on several occasions. After the hitch, I went straight to the ship's sick bay for a pain relieving injection and after a day's rest, and having 'spat out' the pebble, I was fit to fly again.

During this stage we began to cover the interceptor ready deck (ILC) watch to repel possible air strikes or intercept enemy scouts, with two aircraft within five minutes of catapulting and armed with AIM-9B Sidewinder missiles and 20mm guns. Also ready were four aircraft with six Mk 82 bombs and a reserve aircraft with a Chaff launcher system for electronic deception, all at 30 minutes warning.

The eighth aircraft was configured with an in-flight refuelling tank to be catapulted in case of need, as we were operating without an alternative airfield on the ground. This meant that the fuel was what was needed to get to the target and back to the carrier, and in case we could not hook up, to receive fuel from the tanker aircraft to reach an alternate or to have more attempts at the ship.

The twelve of us pilots were formed in two groups of six to cover these watches and we did it alternately for one day and during daylight hours, as we had no systems for night attacks. We could only, in this case, be catapulted into the last hour of darkness to carry out a mission during the morning twilight. Among those who did not cover the actual guard, flying in the 'Chaff' and tanker planes was foreseen, as well as the position of landing officer signalman.

The air communications plans with the Southern airfields on the mainland and the Islands, together with the approach sectors for each landing field, IFF identification codes, daily code changes for the recognition of our own units, different frequencies and bands, etc., made the communications panorama between the Argentine units quite confusing, which in turn was not fully coordinated with the Naval Forces in the area of operations. In our knee notebook we kept all the variants, but it was still a complex number of pages.

So on 1 May, when the British attacks on Port Stanley began, in the afternoon, in the face of unknown contacts from the air defence radars, the first ILCs took off. These contacts turned out to be Air Force Canberra aircraft returning to the mainland without linking up with the Naval Force or activating the IFF, which was quite logical for those who had been engaged in combat and also suffered losses.

The Aircraft Carrier Task Force was located in an area east of Puerto Deseado some 120 miles from the coast and these types of alarms were always repeated for the same reason, that they were radar contacts caused by Argentine aircraft in transit from the mainland to the islands or on their return without establishing communications.

Also that first of May in the afternoon, a Tracker on a scout mission detected seven estimated targets of the enemy Task Force, and the aircraft carrier with its escort ships set course for that position to launch the attack with our aircraft. The targets were out of range for our six-bomb configuration and mostly low-flying airfoil.

The sun was setting at 18:00 and we had to wait to make the attack in the morning twilight.

Again, the enemy Naval Force was spotted at 23:00 hours by another Tracker. Six A-4Qs with four Mk 82 bombs were enlisted and I would lead the attack, keeping one aircraft in reserve and one as a tanker for the return. By tables of probability, considering British anti-aircraft and counter-aircraft defence, of our six planes, four would get to drop their bombs and only two would return on board. Out of sixteen bombs dropped there was a 25 per cent chance of a hit, or four 500lb bombs. This could neutralize an aircraft carrier and the loss of four aircraft was acceptable.

Shortly after midnight, an enemy scout, believed to be a Sea Harrier, remained within 60nm of the naval force orbiting for 30 minutes as a signal that it was maintaining contact with our carrier group.

The attack would no longer be a surprise; they would be expecting us with all their units on high alert, as I was able to confirm years later. Moreover, the enemy force was not supporting a landing on the islands as originally believed and therefore had freedom of action.

During the night the wind began to die down, which was unusual in that area, and the expected distance during the early morning from the targets was more than 250nm. The weight of the aircraft had to be reduced so that they could be catapulted with little real wind. The variable was the bombs, as the fuel was what was needed to accomplish the mission.

Near the time of catapulting the wind was zero and only one bomb could be carried by each aircraft. The probability of impact was reduced to only one bomb out of four dropped. The higher command decided that the anticipated loss of own aircraft and the low probability of success did not justify the operation and that the aircraft were reserved for another favourable opportunity.

The war had only just begun, but that opportunity from the carrier was not repeated. That afternoon the cruiser *General Belgrano* was sunk by a nuclear-powered submarine launching conventional torpedoes beyond the detection range of our anti-submarine warfare escort ships. There was no doubt that our positions were known to the enemy through various sources of information, and the ships had to withdraw to shallower water areas to avoid nuclear submarine attacks.

On 9 May the Squadron disembarked from the aircraft carrier, and the transfer of all the necessary support to be able to operate from the Almirante Quijada Naval Air Base in Río Grande began. On 12 May, the first division of aircraft was transferred, and on 13 May I did the same, after my aircraft had failed the day before.

During that navigation, with flight plans reserved, we were lucky not to collide with a twin-engine civilian aircraft, which, flying on the opposite course and at the same level, crossed between the aircraft of our formation halfway between Bahía Blanca and Viedma.

From 14 May we began to cover the guard with six aircraft in attack configuration armed with four Mk 82 bombs and 20mm guns. One aircraft was to be a reserve and the other was configured as a tanker, to go out to help in case of a fuel emergency, as we were operating at the limit of the action radius. Unfortunately the tanker broke down a few days later, in an accident on a parking platform and we could not count on the system for the rest of the campaign. The inconveniences from Río Grande were many, at that time of the year and at that latitude. Forty per cent of the days there were adverse operating conditions due to low cloud cover, restricted visibility, out-of-bounds crosswinds on their only runway, icing on the runway, etc. This was often set against the weather situation in the Falkland Islands. Daylight hours were few and that was compounded by the one-hour time difference from the Falkland Islands, which meant that it would get dark an hour earlier at that longitude.

Information on enemy positions was scarce and out of date, arriving almost two hours later due to the delays of the shore operation, the distance sailed and in-flight refuelling. Operating from the aircraft carriers closest to the Islands, the Sea Harriers had control of the air, and the presence of the CAPs increased on the arrival of the Argentine attacking aircraft, possibly due to information relayed by infiltrators in the take-off area from the mainland and the collaboration of Chile.

The Puerto Argentino runway could be used in an emergency for a landing, but its short length meant that it was not suitable for high-performance aircraft. There was also no positive radar control from the island, due to the low-flying conditions both during the attack and the withdrawal, which prevented communications. There was only information from enemy PACs in the area and this information was received by relay aircraft which, out of range of the enemy, could receive the information and transmit it to the attackers in low-level flight.

The time spent in the area of operations was minimal due to the great distance to be sailed, and the possibility of a rescue in the event of the aircraft being abandoned beyond 150 miles from the coast was minimal.

The patrol vessel *Alférez Sobral* had been attacked while on a mission to rescue the crew of an Air Force Canberra on 1 May, and some time later an Argentine Army helicopter was shot down when it heroically attempted to rescue the shipwrecked crew of the fishing boat *Narwal*. Survival at sea at those latitudes, even with an anti-exposure suit and an equipped dinghy, is highly improbable.

In Río Grande, we occupied a pilots' room in the hangar, where the crews remained on duty with the pre-flight in general and then updated with the data of the ordered mission. From early in the morning, I was in radio contact – through cryptophonic equipment – with the higher command at the Espora Base, and I received the orders to attack. At night, he returned to the underground operations centre to communicate the general news of the day.

With Lieutenant Commander Jorge Colombo, who was the commander of the Super Étendard, we would listen to what we called 'The Master's Voice' twice a day. Then there was an officer on duty who answered calls and called us for important events.

A week after we were enlisted, on 21 May, the British landed at San Carlos; but when we were ordered on our first mission that day, it was still not clear what was happening.

The order was 'Attack ships in the San Carlos Strait, off Port San Carlos. Number of ships 4/5. Position not determined. Tanker aircraft for return if necessary and Argentine Air Force CAP in the area.'

The weather at Río Grande was good, as were the alternatives on the mainland. The area of operations indicated 6/7 octaves of Stratus at 300/400m with visibility-reducing showers and medium to high cloud layers. Before take-off we were given further information that there could be between nine and twelve ships.

At 1015 hours 3-A-301 took off with Frigate Lieutenant Alejandro Olmedo and Lieutenant Marco Benitez as the numbered ships and 10 minutes later the second section, made up of Lieutenant Commander Carlos Zubizarreta, Lieutenant Commander Felix Médici and Lieutenant Commander Carlos Oliveira, took off.

This separation in time was due to the fact that we occupied the runway width with three aircraft and after the first take-off, the other aircraft would taxi to the headland to carry out the manoeuvre, as they could not be on the runway behind those taking off, due to the danger of ingesting some foreign element in the turbine, propelled by the exhaust of the engines at 100 per cent during the take-off run of the preceding aircraft.

Nor could we delay in rendezvous after the formation take-off, because with full fuel we were in marginal conditions to make the navigation to the distant islands some 400 miles away, carry out the attack and withdrawal in low flight from 100 miles from the target with the high fuel consumption that this means, and return to the landing with some margin of fuel reserve.

Because of this rush to use as little fuel as possible on the ground, from turbine start-up to take-off, and given that the A-4 has no battery, during the taxi I had to programme the VFL Omega navigation system at the same time as carrying out the corresponding checks on the aircraft and its armament. In that first experience with the equipment, although I had practiced it on the ground, I must have made a mistake in the data entry, which after take-off meant that the navigator did not work.

Captain Zubizarreta's navigator didn't work either and I had to navigate with the tail bearing of the Río Grande radio aids.

Fulfilling the flight profile according to the distance estimated by speed and time, in the absence of a navigator, within the estimated 100 miles of the Islands, we began to fly low over the sea, but without a reliable bearing, since at that altitude we were not receiving signals from Río Grande.

We were flying below very low broken cloud cover with snow showers making visibility difficult. When I spotted the low coast of the Islands, believing that I was landing on Soledad Island in the area of Islas Pelada and Aguila, I began to fly along what I estimated to be the San Carlos Strait. After several minutes without sighting any targets, we reached the minimum amount of fuel necessary to return and made a wide right turn over the island. Heading towards Río Grande I saw the ship *Carcarañá* anchored near the coast and then the ship *Bahía Buen Suceso* on the opposite coast and further south.

After more than two hours of flying, frustrated at not having seen the possible targets and with minimal fuel, we landed with the four Mk 82 bombs in the launcher. This was the number of bombs we could carry at maximum take-off weight with a full load of fuel.

Now the information about the situation was a little more precise and the next mission that day was 'Attack damaged ship off Fox Bay and if the first section is successful, the second section will continue through the San Carlos Strait to locate the ships and attack'. This was later modified to 'Attack the ships near Puerto San Carlos. S-2 aircraft at the mouth of the San Carlos Strait for guidance between 14:00 and 15:00'.

The weather situation in the area of operations was 4/5 octaves of Stratus at 500/600me with isolated showers and medium to high cloud cover. It had improved somewhat for attacks, but also made the aircraft more vulnerable to the presence of enemy CAPs in the Area of Operations.

The pilots of the second flight were waiting ready to depart once the aircraft were refuelled and work was done on both navigators to check their operation. We relayed our experiences to them and shortly after 14:00 the two sections departed within 15 minutes of each other.

In the first section were Lieutenant Commander Jorge Philippi, Frigate Lieutenant Marcelo Márquez and Naval Lieutenant José Arca. The second section was made up of Navy Lieutenants Benito Rótolo, Carlos Lecour and Roberto Sylvester.

In the operations room with the information of the Argentine ships I had sighted, I was able to determine that I had actually made landfall on Gran Malvina Island, passing through the Colon Channel and San Julian Bay. On the right turn I entered back through the San Carlos Strait south of Port Howard. There the sighted ships were near Port Fox.

While I was preparing the mission report I followed the division's flight alternatives. Of the six aircraft that had departed, only the three from the second section were returning. They had listened to the communications of the first section when they made their attack and later when they warned that they were under attack, and to the leader of the first section who reported that he was ejecting.

From Puerto Argentino we were informed that Lieutenant Arca had been rescued after ejecting from his plane, which had arrived at the airfield with major damage, but could not land due to missing parts of the landing gear. After ejection he fell into the water in the bay and from there was rescued by an Army helicopter piloted by the then Captain Svendsen, who had to sink one of the aircraft's skis into the water as a last resort to get the pilot out of the water, as he had no rescue winch.

From Lieutenant Arca we learned that the section, after attacking a Type 21 frigate, had been intercepted by Harrier aircraft. He received cannon fire; he confirmed that Captain Philippi had reported that he ejected when his plane was hit by a missile, and that he did not know about Lieutenant Márquez's plane. He had only seen a parachute, but could not say whose it was.

That night I had one of my saddest tasks; to tell Graciela and her children – who lived in Río Grande, as it was Captain Philippi's original destination that year – of his disappearance in combat, although I conveyed my hope because a parachute had been observed. Someone in Mar del Plata was serving a similar commission with the family of Lieutenant Márquez.

Lieutenant Rótolo's section had also attacked a Type 21 frigate in the vicinity of Ruiz Puente Bay in the San Carlos Strait. From subsequent information, statements by the ship's commander and detailed investigations, there is no doubt that the result of the attack by both sections was the end of the frigate HMS *Ardent*.

We also learned after the conflict who shot down Lieutenant Márquez, that his aircraft exploded in mid-air when hit by 30mm shells and months later, that that pilot, Flight Lieutenant John Leeming, on 23 February 1983 lost his life when his Harrier collided with a similar one while practising air combat manoeuvres at 10,000ft over his base in England.

Captain Philippi would turn up four days after crashing in the San Carlos Strait, swimming ashore, surviving on Soledad Island and finally being found by the manager of an estancia in the area, who, after sheltering him, radioed Puerto Argentino with the news, from where they would go to retrieve him by helicopter.

he next mission was on 23 May, and the order read 'Attack ships in Puerto San Carlos, undetermined number, after in-flight refuelling with KC-130 in position: 52° 30' South, 66° 00' West at 1300 hours. The attack will follow that of the Argentine Air Force. Target Primary Material Ships and Secondary Material Port and Facilities.'

The weather at Río Grande was not good; there was a strong crosswind on the runway and the runway was wet with light drizzle from the Nimbus Stratus covering the sky at 800m. Cloud tops were over 7,500m. For the area of operations the forecast was good and Port Stanley was reporting enemy combat air patrols in arc over Soledad Island.

This time I was accompanied by Lieutenant Marco Benitez, Lieutenant Commander Carlos Zubizarreta and Lieutenant Carlos Oliveira. I flew in 3-A-301 equipped with VFL-Omega and left the runway at 12:35. After a wide turn to rendezvous, before entering cloud, I set course for the coordinated point over the sea to meet the Air Force tanker.

The missions on the 21st had practically shown us the need to refuel, although in theory we were coming in at the limit, and this was yet another variable in flight planning. I started the climb into the clouds with the four planes close together so as not to lose sight of each other and luckily the navigator was working properly. After crossing 7,500m we emerged from the cloud.

Arriving at the refuelling point I contacted the KC-130 aircraft and they confirmed that they were 120 miles to the east of the planned refuelling point and that they were flying at 4,000m. Thanks to the navigation system I was able to redirect my course. I then began a descent to reach 4,000m where the refuelling aircraft were flying through layers of cloud. In order to accomplish the mission, we had to fill the underwing tanks. We started refuelling in sections in each of the two KC-130s.

The manoeuvre consisted of flying at the speed of the Hercules aircraft, from which the approximately 50ft long hose with a funnel-like basket at the end was detached from the under-wing refuelling system.

Approaching from behind the aircraft with low relative speed between the two, the A-4's probe was inserted into the basket and automatically sealed and the fuel could be delivered. The probe is the small tubular shuttle at the front of the aircraft.

We performed this manoeuvre with the A-4s equipped with a tank under the fuselage in case of need, but we had also practiced it with the KC-130. For those who are used to formation flying and appreciate the relative movements well, the manoeuvre is not difficult, except that sometimes the aerodynamic turbulence caused by the tanker aircraft affects the receiver and complicates the hook-up.

Lieutenant Oliveira's plane had a failure in the fuel reception system and after repeated unsuccessful attempts at manoeuvres, I ordered him to return to Río Grande, as he did not have enough fuel for the entire mission.

I updated my new position and the three planes started the navigation to the Islands, more precisely to the landfall point which was San José Island west of Gran Malvina. Before 100 miles from the target we flew low over the sea with the radar altimeter set at 15m so that its alarm would warn us if we went below this height. This was not the case, but flying over a calm sea with no reference points you lose the sense of visual depth and this is dangerous so close to the water.

Once over Gran Malvina Island, I started to fly low over the bright green and desolate terrain due to the humidity, which would take me to the area of elevations on the east side of the island and in front of Puerto San Carlos to hide us from the radars behind the hills in that sector. During this phase I communicated with the Air Force plane that was relaying communications and requested updated information on the targets and the presence of enemy CAPs. At that moment, an Air Force pilot was on the frequency and reported after the attack that one A-4 had been shot down, another was damaged, a third had not launched and the fourth was unharmed. They belonged to Captain Pablo Carballo's squadron which had preceded us that day in the attack on the ships in the bay. The targets were in the strait and in the bay of Puerto de San Carlos.

Heading east I ordered my numerals to accelerate to 450 knots, select armament and wished them luck! I climbed a little to pass the side of the 450m Mount Rosalia and could see the coast of Isla Soledad and the entrance to the bay. It was high as I left the coast and with stick ahead and some negative Gs I brought the plane up to 300ft.

The sea looked calm; the first vessel I spotted was a frigate in the middle of the bay sailing towards the exit and I could see that it had a helicopter on the stern. I started my firing run from a long way off towards the target and up to that point it all looked like an attack exercise so often repeated with the Sea Fleet. The only difference was when the sky began to fill with black smoke from the explosions of anti-aircraft shells and machine-gun tracers. I could tell that the ship was firing with its forward gun and from the volume of fire it was not the only one doing so. I was then able to observe other units outside and inside the bay.

It would take me a little less than a minute to go through the strait and before I reached the mouth of the bay I could see a large logistic-type vessel on the north side of the bay with its bow pointing south, but not sailing, which immediately became my target as it was more profitable. Our priority was the aircraft carriers, then the logistics ships, and then the frigates or destroyers.

The calmness in the air had disappeared, it was turbulent and I don't know if it was because of the wind over the high coast or because of the anti-aircraft fire. With my sights set on the target I saw a kind of flare from the bow of the ship moving erratically towards me.

I recognized it as a missile and fell sharply to the right. Out of the corner of my eye I had the sensation of something passing my left and I violently fell onto the attack course. The sight was passing the bow of the ship and I dropped my bombs. The aircraft freed from the ton of explosives reared up and as I began evasive manoeuvres, turning this way and that, while 'sticking' to the water, I heard the detonations of my salvo. To my right I was leaving a black-painted transport ship, while I made a wide turn to the north to protect myself by flying low over the terrain.

When I again found the sea to the north of Solitude Island, I set a westerly course, maintaining my low flight at 450 knots.

My heart was disturbed: there was a large, ship-like silhouette in front of me, which I could not make out well because of the sun, but there were no friendly ships in the area and I had only 20mm guns that would surely jam in the first burst. I knew its name later: it was Roca Remolinos, which rises several metres out of the sea. I heard over the radio the voices of my two numerals who had also survived the flak and were rallying. They sounded happy.

For me, another problem began: the fuel gauge was reading low and this was a sign that the external fuel tanks had not transferred normally. I tried transfer through the wing by-pass with no results and then launched the emergency generator, as a last resort, but the fuel was not transferring.

It was dangerous to climb so soon because of the possible presence of enemy interceptors, but I had no alternative but to comply with a flight profile used in emergency cases called 'Fouled Deck Range', when an alternative must be reached from the sea because of the impossibility of hooking on to the carrier.

I launched all the external charges by means of the lever that explodes cartridges that eject the sub-wing tanks and the MER launcher, at the same time as I began the ascent to 40,000ft with the aircraft aerodynamically clean.

Captain Zubizarreta together with Lieutenant Benitez were already heading for Río Grande and wanted to accompany me, but I refused as I had to fly a flight profile very neatly and I preferred to do it alone so as not to complicate the manoeuvre. When I levelled off I had 1,100lbs of fuel and was about 250 miles from the airfield. Normally this was the fuel that was used for landing and I should have had about 2,300lbs at that point in normal operation. What followed was a succession of data given to me by the navigator. At times the fuel was just enough to land and at times it wasn't, it was all a function of the wind at altitude which was the variable. If I didn't make it, I would have to eject over the sea. I still had about 100 miles to go when the other planes switched to tower frequency for landing and I didn't hear them again.

At about 60 miles I started the descent on idle and asked control to guide me by radar to the end of the runway for a direct high caution approach.

I was entering instruments at 7,000m and was to exit cloud with the runway ahead and the correct altitude. The VLF navigator together with the controller allowed me to reach that point. There I lowered the landing gear and that's when I switched to the control tower frequency. The tower told me to land on the right-hand side of the runway. When I asked why, they did not answer me, and only repeated that I should use the right half of the runway.

The wind was a crosswind, the runway was wet and these were not good conditions for the A-4. When I landed I could see a crashed A-4 on the left side of the runway, which was resting on its nose and without the cockpit. I lowered the hook of the aircraft and grabbed the cable armed in the middle of the runway; this system reduced the speed of the A-4 and then cut off. Once the run was under control, I raised the hook to taxi to the parking area. When I cut the engine on the apron, my fuel gauge read 200lbs, less than I would have needed if I had had to escape and make another circuit.

Tragic news awaited me: Lieutenant Commander Carlos Zubizarreta had died. On the landing run, with the bombs in his launcher, because he was unable to drop them during the attack due to system failures, aircraft 3-A-306 blew the left landing gear tyre and began to drift to that side. Anticipating the runway departure and as the procedures manual advises in these cases, he began ejection. He blew the cockpit, the rocket-propelled seat came out but did not climb high enough to allow the whole sequence to be completed in time, and the parachute deployed the instant he hit the ground. The ejector rocket was still burning slowly and with a lot of black smoke. It was one of the rockets that had expired and been extended for operations. That same night we paid him funeral honours as an F-28 loaded his coffin for transport to Bahía Blanca where Ana and her children were waiting for him with the Navy authorities.

Years later I was able to confirm which ship he had unsuccessfully attacked on 23 May. It was the amphibious assault ship HMS *Intrepid*, which although it did not shoot me down with the manually guided Sea Cat missile, it did its job by knocking me off target when the bombs were dropped, leaving me with a long salvo.

Lieutenant Marco Benitez, who followed me in the formation, continued his run and dropped three bombs (the fourth failed) on the Type 21 frigate HMS *Antelope*, and did not hear the explosions of his bombs. On the ground he would tell me that he saw no less than two missiles pass close to the tail of my aircraft, coming from land, possibly from the Rapier system, which I had not seen. *Antelope* had also been attacked by Captain Pablo Carballo's squadron and hit with a 1,000lb bomb on her starboard side by First

Lieutenant Guadagnini, who lost his life in this action. The frigate sank on 24 May after an attempt to defuse one of the two bombs she had received resulted in it exploding, causing uncontrollable fires and the subsequent explosion of her stern, which broke her in two. That image went around the world as it was captured in a dramatic photograph.

May 25th brought us good news; Captain Philippi had been recovered, a Super Étendard had sunk the container ship *Atlantic Conveyor* and the Air Force had sunk the destroyer *Coventry*.

On those nights, civilian personnel from the Central Naval Aircraft Workshop painted the remaining four Skyhawks in green and brown to camouflage them according to the terrain of the Islands, as the original colour intended for operations at sea was very conspicuous on land.

The British had established a foothold on the islands, maintained air dominance and their counter-air defences were entrenched. Our aircraft continued to operate in sections for the rest of the conflict and completed their last mission on 12 June, as the scheduled sortie for the 14th was cancelled due to the fall of Port Stanley.

These missions with attacks on land installations were in many cases aborted due to the presence of enemy CAPs in the area and in other cases their success was relative.

It was my 40th birthday on 14 June and that night the eight of us pilots had dinner in a restaurant in Río Grande. We were accompanied by the then Frigate Lieutenant Diego Goñi, who had joined the Squadron a few days earlier to fly maintenance flights only, because he did not have the necessary training to carry out combat missions. There was also Technical Lieutenant Commander Hector Vite, who was in charge of aircraft maintenance, and my good friend Eduardo Blau, a former aviator pilot and at that time a Boing 737 commander, who had arranged his commercial flight to visit me on that occasion. He, like so many other Aerolineas Argentinas pilots, had flown troops to the Falklands Islands until mid-April, when the exclusion zone was declared.

Many former naval pilots in that situation had visited us to give us moral support, among them my colleagues Jorge Badih and Jorge Dejean. A few days earlier we had also received a visit from the then naval aviator Captain Máximo Rivero Kelly, who was not in the command line due to his duties that year, but he offered us all his experience and support for our task with the greatest understanding, as did the then Naval Captain Héctor Martini, who was the most senior aviator officer in the area.

The conflict was over and we were filled with mixed feelings. Three months had passed since the first embarkation on aircraft carriers for a training stage and from that moment on we had not taken a break; the events were accelerating and the growing activity was involving us more and more. From the joy of taking the Falklands to the disappointment of defeat, a little more than 70 days had passed, but a lifetime for us. Many acquaintances and friends from all the Forces suddenly left an empty place. Whoever occupied a bed, a place at the table, from one day to the next no longer did so. They were physically absent forever. We knew what we were exposing ourselves to, and only an unconscious person could say that he was not afraid. The essential thing was to master it, to live with it, but to overcome it. During the missions, there was no time to think about anything other than the mission itself. Flight planning, ground operations, navigation, were stages that we carried out routinely and with all our senses focused on them.

The attack only differed from training because of the anti-aircraft fire, but in those few seconds the concentration was total, there was no time to think about anything else. Anxiety manifested itself on the ground, in my case I slept little and lost weight. As Commander I also had responsibilities over my pilots and mechanics that went beyond my own demands. I think that night of the 14th we were overwhelmed by the frustration of the unwanted end and perhaps the relief at the end of the anxiety. A parishioner from another table invited us with a few bottles of wine, in homage to the fact that we had fought, but society in general, swept up in the criticism of the military government, ignored us. Our return was inglorious; there were reproaches of all kinds, uninformed criticism and general despondency.

A few days later I had another operation on my left arm to remove the arm plaster, and at the end of August a medical board determined that I could continue flying despite the 30 per cent incapacity for work caused by the restrictions on my arm. Back with my family, I realized that I valued much more the simple and almost inconsequential facts of life that I had not previously considered. I had a different outlook and a different attitude to what I thought no longer represented what was really important and what perhaps used to keep me awake at night.

Shortly afterwards, I received the Argentinean Navy's 'Honour for Valour in Combat' award for 'As Commander of the Third Air and Naval Fighter and Attack Squadron, participating in a physically handicapped condition due to a previous aviation accident, setting a permanent example to his subordinates'.

This would also be recognized by the decoration 'La Nación Argentina al Valor en Combate' by decree and received the recognition of the Congress of Combatants.

Those of us who were part of the Squadron at that time, and with our wives from that moment onwards, meet annually on the date close to 21 May, our baptism of fire, to remember the actions and pay homage to our dead. We know that also in Great Britain, the former commander of the *Ardent* meets with his crew for the same purpose on a similar date.

During the months of September and October there was little flying activity and we only carried out one exercise with the Brazilian Navy operating from the *25 de Mayo*. During that period I reached 260 hitches, and that would be my last activity on the much-loved ship.

Towards the end of the year, Lieutenant Commander Roberto Loubet Jambert lost his life in an accident in 3-A-306 while flying at night, perhaps due to spatial disorientation. The A-4 was the same one that Captain Zubizarreta was flying when he ejected at Río Grande and had been recovered during the month of June by the personnel of the Central Naval Aircraft Workshop. It must be one of the few cases in which the same single-seat aircraft is a common factor in the death of two pilots. On 2 November I had made my last A-4 flight in it and at the end of that month I took over command of the First A-4.

Commander Castro Fox:

On Sunday 9 August 1981 I was catapulted aboard A-4Q 3-A-303 on a very calm afternoon. I was re-qualifying and had already completed two hook-ups on 3-A-307 during the morning.

'Stable deck, wind 28/30 knots'. The voice of the signalman radioed me the conditions for landing on the aircraft carrier *25 de Mayo*.

'03, ball, three five,' was my reply as I watched the yellow light indication projected by the stabilized system indicating the approach slope of the ship's port side. At the same time I confirmed the number of hundreds of pounds of fuel in the aircraft.

I completed my basic turn to face the final leg with 500ft of altitude and down to the left was the white wake of the ship contrasting with an almost calm blue-green sea. Ahead, a thick inverted 'T' painted yellow indicated the start of the runway angled at 8 degrees to the aircraft carrier's centreline and on its right, the 'island' full of balconies, antennae and the ship's smokestack from which a column of smoke rose and rapidly aligned itself to the relative wind, running parallel to the axis of the angled runway.

My attention was distributed in keeping the 'ball' centred with respect to the green reference line materialized by spotlights on its sides, the angle of attack indicator at 'Donna' with the yellow traffic light and the alignment with respect

3-A-330 after it was recovered, it was a total loss. (*CANA*)

Two images of Lt Cdr Castro Fox A-4Q in which he had an accident being badly wounded. (*CANA*)

to the runway axis that was shifting slightly to the right due to the movement of the ship.

Smooth throttle movements and flight controls kept the references, and the engine at 80 to 90 percent of its 8,200lbs of thrust.

The high stern of the ship rocked slowly and the high-pitched noise of the turbine was broken by the Signal Officer's directions over the radio.

I had over 250 hitches to my credit, but the attention and tension was as usual. There is no opportunity for carelessness; it is only after the flight that one can recreate the memory and take comfort in this intense activity so dear to naval aviators.

The aircraft carrier was rapidly increasing in size; I crossed her stern at 130 knots of speed and with a centred ball I reached the area of the six brake lines. When I touched the deck, I mechanically moved the throttle to 100 per cent with my left hand and at the same time, with the thumb of my left hand, activated the 'switch' to engage the dive brake so that I could take off again in case the aircraft did not engage.

Simultaneously, the plane began to decelerate. I had taken the number three cable, on the runway axis, and my body was restrained by the straps that secured me to the seat across my torso, while my head moved freely forward.

The nose of the plane, now low, shuddered with oscillating lateral movements as a result of the great deceleration as the 14,500lbs of the plane's weight came to a stop at a relative speed of 100 knots in a distance of less than 60m.

In front of me was the ocean, separated by just a few feet of deck.

Suddenly, when I was at very low speed and reducing the throttle to the minimum, my body pressed against the back of the seat and my head slammed into the seat cushion. The plane had broken free of the cable when the cable was cut and was accelerating. Instinctively I brought the throttle to the one hundred percent position out of a habit I had acquired on the touch-and-go or 'bolters' on deck, because I was accelerating.

This time I did not have enough speed to take off again, as had happened to me four years earlier with this same aircraft, and I immediately reduced the throttle again while putting my right foot down to try to bring it towards the axis of the axial runway and have more space to try to slow it down. There I would have about 50m more cover, but the speed was too much to slow it down and the plane was skidding towards the port side. I heard the voice of the signalman shouting over the radio 'Eject – Eject!' and my reaction was instinctive: with my right hand I pulled the lower lever of the ejection seat, felt a dull explosion behind me and the cockpit, triggered by the cartridge I had fired, slid backwards, and now, I thought, I would be pushed out of the seat by the rocket, but the seat did not come out.

The plane continued its run towards the end of the angled runway; the nose wheel dipped into the balcony of that sector and the plane passed over a 40mm anti-aircraft mount, at the same time turning sharply to the left as the wheel on that side was the first to lose contact with the runway.

I could no longer see the canopy; I was falling into the sea from 13m with the plane upside down and tightly attached to the ejection seat by the upper and lower straps. Not five seconds had elapsed since the cable had been cut, and I was losing consciousness when I hit the water.

All these actions and images, from the moment I recognized the emergency when the cable was cut, I remember them vividly in a time that passes as if in slow motion until the plane falls into the sea in the late afternoon.

It is from the moment when I was being transferred in a Sea King helicopter at night to the Naval Hospital in Puerto Belgrano, some 100 miles away, that I began to regain consciousness and I even thought that, tied as I was to the stretcher, I had little chance of surviving a splashdown that night.

What happened after I hit the sea I later learned from the accounts of all the protagonists, but I have not been able to recall any of those moments.

When the plane hit the water in a nose-down and inverted position, the seat ejection took place and I must have gone out like a torpedo towards the bottom of the sea propelled by the rocket that was ignited at that moment. Otherwise I would have met the fate of the plane, heading for the bottom of the ocean.

The state of my left arm was evidence of the force with which the seat left the plane. I had my left hand on the throttle, which is a serious error in ejection, and my forearm suffered the consequences of coming out between the inner side of the cabin and the side surface of the seat, which leaves little space. As a result, I suffered fractures of the ulna, radius and trochlea, as well as scapulohumeral dislocation.

The seat continued, through the various explosive cartridges, with its sequence that unlocks the strap to the torso, inflates the bladders to separate me from the seat and initiates the exit of the parachute extractor pylon. Had this sequence failed, I would have continued to the bottom of the sea strapped to the seat.

Dressed as I was, in an anti-exposure suit that retains air between the body and the fabric, plus the rest of the flight gear: torso, survival waistcoat and anti-G still dry, my body began a slow ascent to the surface by positive buoyancy.

Those who saw me appear on the surface after almost two minutes said that I was right-handed, as I had a broken left arm. Immediately the Alouette at the rescue station and commanded by the then Lieutenant Commander Carlos Espilondo approached my position and two swimmers jumped into the sea, and after detaching my parachute, passed the rescue sling under my shoulders.

I was hoisted up by the helicopter's winch at the same time as he began his transfer, but I didn't go with him for long: unconscious and with a dislocated shoulder, my arms rose up and let the sling slide, and I fell back into the sea. This time the frogmen had to swim to my new position, and when they arrived, pull me out from under the surface, because with the wet gear I no longer had positive buoyancy and they had made the mistake of not inflating my lifejacket. The sling was attached to the carabiner that is worn on the flight torso and this time I was hoisted onto the Alouette.

When they deposited me on the flight deck, the first manoeuvre was to remove all the water that was inside me and quickly I was taken by the bow lift on the flight deck on a stretcher to the operating theatre.

On the way I suffered my first cardiorespiratory arrest, from which I was resuscitated. For a long time I was unresponsive to external stimuli, and in the operating theatre I suffered my second cardiorespiratory arrest, from which I was also recovered. A few days later, the doctors asked me if I remembered how I had recovered from these arrests. When I said no, they were relieved.

I had polytrauma, immersion asphyxia, lung shock, cardiorespiratory arrest, skull trauma with loss of consciousness, biorbital trauma, fracture of the radial ulna and left rib, left anterior glenohumeral dislocation, submental, supreauricular and left palperal injuries, bipalperal haematoma, bilateral conjunctival echiomosis with loss of consciousness, bilateral conjunctival echiomosis and multiple abrasions, as reported in the accident report by the then Lieutenant Commander Edgar Coria, who had treated me together with the doctors of the naval air group. That night I was admitted to the Intensive Care ward of the Hospital, where I would remain for four days.

At midnight, Lieutenant Commander Jorge Philippi and Graciela, his wife, called the flat where we lived in Bahía Blanca to inform Stella of my accident and hospitalisation. A few months later it would be me who would tell Graciela of her husband's disappearance during the Malvinas conflict.

My appearance must have been really unpleasant, with oedemas, effusions, stitches, etc., and that is what I concluded when I noticed that those who visited me in Intensive Care and who were not doctors, soon left pale. The nurses did not want, with puerile excuses, to provide me with a mirror that I asked for several times to see myself.

Even days later, when my children were able to visit me in a common room, they were really shocked. If any of them were thinking of going into medicine, I think I frustrated their career.

Among the factors that helped me survive the possible neurological after-effects of the accident, according to the specialists, were the cold of the water and the fact that I was breathing 100 per cent oxygen during the flight. The A-4 does not have an on-demand system that mixes oxygen into the cabin air, but a liquid oxygen system with its converter and regulator that provides pure oxygen. But I think that the 'Tata Dios' did not foresee me on that day or he made a mistake in the San Pedro list.

Having overcome the major risk of possible pulmonary or renal complications, the ordeal of recovering my left arm began. Operated with pins in both bones of the forearm, I was given a plaster cast that I would wear for more than three months, modifying my posture, size, etc.

Declared unfit to fly, every two months I went to the Medical Examination Board, which reported on my recovery without sequelae from the various traumatisms, abrasions, interstitial pneumonitis, etc., but my left arm was still affected and in such a way that there were great restrictions on movement.

I went to the Squadron to perform the duties of Second-in-Command, but watched with envy how the rest of the pilots flew.

Towards the end of the year, the awards for the 1980 weapons exercises were presented at a ceremony held in the Assembly Hall of the Puerto Belgrano Naval Base. It was my turn to go up to receive the award from the Rosario newspaper *La Capital*, for the best individual annual average in air gunnery among all the attack squadron pilots. On seeing me with my arm in plaster, someone jokingly remarked 'What would it have been like with both arms!'

In the first days of December 1981 and a week after taking off the plaster cast, I took command of the Third Naval Fighter and Attack Squadron. With my left hand I had difficulty holding my sword during the ceremony in which Lieutenant Commander Jorge A. Philippi handed over the command to me to go to the Río Grande Base.

The condition of the aircraft equipment was as bad as mine physically. In the last months of operation, cracks had appeared in the intermediate wing spar, detected in November when, after a hitch on the aircraft carrier, 3-A-306 began to lose fuel on the flight deck from the landing gear nacelle. When the ten aircraft were inspected, it turned out that seven had a cracked landing gear strut, and they were transferred to the Central Naval Aircraft Workshop for repair. This was a major job, which would consist of replacing the wing. Of the three aircraft remaining in service without cracks, one was due for a major inspection from January and another from March, work which had been in the workshop for some three months.

To make matters worse, the MK-1 Mod 0 ejection seat booster cartridges installed were all due to expire on 30 December of that year and due to the so-called Humprey-Kennedy Amendment, the United States would not deliver the cartridges we had sent to be flown early enough for replacement. The delayed ejection I had in August of that year could be a sign that they were at the end of their life. Thanks to a loan from the Argentine Air Force, we had three ejectable cartridges from January 1982.

Also, of the twelve pilots in the Squadron, four were new recruits, one was undergoing minimal training and I had no chance of flying until after the operation I was due to undergo in April to remove the arm tutors and the corresponding rehabilitation period. Two of the remaining six pilots had not yet completed their qualification on board the carrier.

Bearing in mind that the incorporation of the Super Étendard was taking up most of the efforts to put them into operation, and that our Squadron would slowly be replaced by them in the tasks of attack and embarked anti-aircraft defence, my demands were justified so that my superiors would not let up in the support of our degraded aircraft, since their lack seriously affected the Navy's capabilities during the transition.

I asked for top priority to be given to repairing the damage to the aircraft with cracks, and in view of the possibility of wing replacements, that these should be with five external stations, like the A-4C models onwards, and with spoilers.

A-4Q 0655/3-A-202 in the United States during training flights. Initially they carried in the callsign '3-', the shield of the Argentine Navy on the rear of the fuselage and in front of the word 'Naval'. Shortly after arriving in Argentina the '3-' was removed and repainted in 1974, when the callsigns also went from 201 to 206 to 301 to 316, the shield was removed and the word 'Naval' was changed to 'Armada'.

Photo aboard the ARA *25 de Mayo* on 14 October 1972, during catapult tests after having verified that there is no impact of the strobe with the LAU-32G rocket pod on the centreline pylon.

3-A-312 being catapulted from the aircraft carrier. This aircraft was lost in combat on 21 May 1982.

A Tercera Escuadrilla Aeronaval de Caza y Ataque A-4Q Skyhawk at Comandante Espora Naval Air Station.

An Mk 82 bomb with Snakeye retarded tail and the inscription 'HMS *Invincible*' in front of A-4Q 3-A-305 aboard *25 de Mayo* on 1 May 1982.

A photo taken in 1983, with *25 de Mayo* with four A-4Qs, three Grumman S-2E Trackers and a Sea King 2-H-235.

HMS *Ardent* after the successful attack by 'Tábano' flight. Minutes later the three Skyhawks were shot down.

Pilots of Tercera Escuadrilla Aeronaval de Caza y Ataque in Río Grande during the war. In the back row: TF Márquez (killed in combat), TN Lecour, RN Oliveira, CC Zubizarreta (killed during the war), CC Philippi, CC Castro Fox, TN Rótolo and TN Benítez. In front: TC Médici, TN Sylvester, TN Arca and TF Olmedo.

Formation of eight A-4Qs seen shortly before the Falklands War, with aircraft 3-A-309, 314, 304, 302, 307, 305, 308 and 301.

3-A-302 on the *25 de Mayo* on 15 October 1982 with Lieutenant Commander Castro Fox at the controls. The following day the Skyhawk was out of service due to structural problems that were repaired after being landed.

The A-4B registration C-222 was painted in an experimental grey scheme during the war, in an attempt to make it less visible over the sea. It was nicknamed 'El tordillo', a name that in Argentina refers to horses with greyish coats.

Lieutenant Juan Arrarás refuelling in flight on 8 June in A-4B registration C-226, with which he would fall in combat on that mission, after being hit by a Sidewinder launched by David Morgan from his Sea Harrier.

During and after the 1982 war, various camouflage schemes were evaluated on A-4Bs, such as this one on C-212, seen on 13 July 1989.

A-4C C-314 refuelling in flight from a Hercules. Since its transfer to V Air Brigade, this aircraft carried the shields of both units.

In the late 1980s, the Argentine Navy tried to buy a small number of A-4N Skyhawks from the Israeli surplus inventory, but the deal fell through and the aircraft were purchased by the Canadian civilian company Top Aces, which mainly uses them as "aggressors" for European air forces, notably the German Luftwaffe. (*Photos: Richard Sánchez*)

During the month of March the first sea stage was carried out, operating our squadron with the three aircraft, two of them extended for the major inspection, in which one pilot was qualified and another four veterans underwent requalification. Ammunition exercises were also carried out in the hangar and on the flight deck before disembarking on 25 March.

On 26 March I was summoned along with the other commanders to a secret meeting with the Commander of Naval Aviation.'

Lieutenant Commander Rodolfo Castro Fox, photographed at Río Grande Naval Air Station during the war.

3-A-302 at Comandante Espora Naval Air Station.

Tercera Escuadrilla maintainers, armourers and plane captains at Río Grande on 26 May 1982. Note the two camouflaged Skyhawks.

The Mk 82 with Snakeye tail was the Tercera Escuadrilla Aeronaval de Caza y Ataque weapon of choice.

Trap of 3-A-305 on the aircraft carrier.

3-A-314 prepares for a departure from the aircraft carrier. This aircraft was lost in combat on 21 May 1982.

A-4Q armed with four LAU-10A pods with four 127mm rockets and six 125kg Mk 81 bombs.

Nine A-4Q Skyhawks seen at the flight line shortly before the Falklands War.

On 18 May 1982 3-A-302 suffered an accident when the nose wheel was retracted. Although the plane was quickly repaired, the Buddy Pack it was carrying was out of service for the rest of the war. It was the only one available to them at the time.

3-A-304 seen at Comandante Espora Naval Air Station.

Aircraft in Río Grande on 20 May 1982, where three Learjets from the Air Force, one Beech B-200 Super King Air, one Fokker F-28 and three A-4Qs from the Navy are seen. Among the Skyhawks is 3-A-307, shot down the next day.

Skyhawks and Super Étendards aboard *25 de Mayo*.

Chapter 7

One-Way Mission

Lieutenant Commander Alberto Jorge Philippi was posted from Tercera Escuadrilla to Río Grande Naval Air Station as its executive officer in January 1982, but upon the Argentine landings near Port Stanley he requested a return to the Escuadrilla where his experience could be employed better.

This is his account of his first and last combat sortie on 21 May 1982.

Our mission when we launched from Río Grande during the afternoon of 21 May was to attack a Royal Navy frigate, supposedly on radar picket duties at the southern end of Falkland Sound or sailing towards this area. Shortly after take-off our command post at Río Grande advised us that we could expect to find Sea Harrier CAPs nearby.

After receiving this new information I thought half amused, how could I be so cool? I was flying a single-engined aircraft over the ocean with a cracked right wing mainspar, a time-expired ejection seat rocket booster, at maximum range with slim chances of being rescued if forced down and knowing that the two 20mm cannon had only a 12 per cent probability of working properly without jamming.

In fact the only thing left to complete this depressing picture was that somebody left a bag full of scorpions in the cockpit!

While taxiing before take-off I had turned on all armament switches, leaving only the master switch off. I knew that sometimes the high stress involved during a run into the target can cause mistakes and I did not want to forget anything.

Armament configuration was the same for our three-ship division (call signs 'Tabano 1' myself; 'Tabano 2' Sub Lieutenant Márquez and 'Tabano 3' Lieutenant Arca). We carried four Mk 82 500lb bombs with Snakeye retarding tails plus 200 rounds for the 20mm guns.

The attack called for a low-level run at 450 knots and at 50ft to avoid radar detection until the last moment. At one nautical mile from the ship we were to climb to 300ft and commence our attack, firing the guns to 'keep their heads down' and waiting until the pipper's dot passed over the bow to pickle the bomb's button.

After delivery we would push the throttle to the firewall and start evasive manoeuvres during the escape leg to avoid being locked by the fire control radars or the SAMs launched against us.

The join-up after take-off was routinely carried out while we climbed to 27,000ft, the planned height for navigating towards the islands. Distance to the target was 385nm with descent starting 100nm away. At 50 miles we should be flying 100ft above the sea. Total flying time to the target area was 58 minutes.

None of the A-4s in our division had navigation computers nor Omega-VL navigation systems, so I worked by magnetic compass and ADF marcations until we started our descent. Once at low level I navigated by dead reckoning and visual references, when I had them taking into account that we were flying at about seven and a half miles per minute.

Then, on the horizon, I saw the islands – five minutes before ETA (Estimated Time of Arrival) – somewhat blurred by low clouds. We obviously had a higher than expected tailwind.

Nobody talked; all our tasks had been dealt with during the preflight briefing, contemplating all possible alternatives. Knowing that they (the British) had very good ECM and ESM, any radio chatter between pilots could mean detection even before entering radar range.

While descending we turned on the master armament switch; now we only had to press the bomb button. We flew by Bird's Island, to the southwest of West Falkland (Gran Malvina), then turned right following the coastline until reaching Cape Meredith. We were flying below the cloud deck, which was approximately at 500ft. Rain showers reduced horizontal visibility to a mile or less, making my wingmen close formation to maintain visual contact.

When we reached Cape Meredith, I ordered a left turn to cross the Sound's southern mouth. Cape Meredith was to our left – tall, dark and menacing – like a bad premonition, its peak covered by clouds while its steep slopes sank into an ocean as dark and menacing as the cape itself.

A chilling though struck me. Visibility was much reduced and if the frigate was in the Sound, her radar would detect us and she could launch her SAMs before we found her. We hadn't a chance, as we didn't have any means of telling if we were 'painted' by hostile fire control radars. The idea of making a 180-degree turn and returning home with my wingman crossed my mind. It was fully justified; in fact the A-4Q division which had launched before us did it.

Nevertheless, I decided to make a short comment over the radio, which reflected the anxiety and stress of those moments – 'It is really long' – referring to the width of the Sound which took some four minutes to cross at our speed. Not finding the feared frigate, I proceed towards the secondary target, British ships in San Carlos Water. So when we overflew the western shores of East Falkland (Soledad) we established an 025-degree heading. Flying at 50ft over the beach with 450 knots on the clock we were going directly to San Carlos, already spread in attack formation.

I was in front in 3-A-307; Lieutenant Márquez in 3-A-314 was behind and to the right, while Lieutenant Arca in 3-A-312 was behind Márquez and to his left. As we went up to the Sound, the weather improved somewhat; the clouds were scattered and we could see a nice blue sky.

Shortly before reaching Grantham Sound we caught sight of the mast and radar antenna of a ship behind Northwest Island, a rock rising from the water near the shore on the northern side of the bay. I signalled to my wingmen the target's location guessing the distance and giving the attack order. My first thought was to attack directly, looking to the rock as cover during our attack run. But I had to change this mode due to the surprising speed with which the ship started to move, leaving from behind the rock and heading into deep water in the Sound. I glanced briefly at the clock; almost three in the afternoon.

'After seeing the ship move, I thought she had detected us. Then I turned right so our formation, could mix with the radar clutter from the shore, flying above it in an easy left turn. I got into a favourable position to attack in a diagonally established run, from the port bow to the starboard bow, thus assuring a maximum impact probability. My wingmen were behind in the formation established before. A last glance to the fuel quantity indicator showed 4,200lbs remaining, about 200lbs above the bingo level. This was based on a 385nm return leg including a 50nm low level escape leg and a 100-knot headwind.

When I calculated mentally that I was at the correct distance, I made a hard left turn, towards the enemy vessel. Thus when I completed the turn I was firmly established on the attack run with approximately a 250-degree heading. I pressed the gun trigger, but after a few rounds both cannons jammed as usual!

Lieutenant Arca, who was flying to my left, could not maintain his inside slot and skidded outside the turn, thus placing his Skyhawk as number two. In order to maintain the formation's integrity Lieutenant Márquez pulled to the left and took Arca's slot as number three. So our faithful Skyhawks made the attack run in the following order: 3-A-307 myself, 3-A-312 Lieutenant Arca and 3-A-314 Lieutenant Márquez. Our 500lb Snakeyes were in a centreline MER [Multiple Ejector Rack]. A planned 250-milliseconds interval, gave the bombs a 40/40m separation. The frigate approximate heading was 225 degrees and she was going at full speed while starting a turn to port. Then we were over her. While on the attack run, and also during the egress, I could see the firing of two missiles [in fact the missiles reported by Philippi were Corvus flare/chaff rockets – Author]. Also I heard one of my wingman say: 'You've hit her sir!'

The nearby Sea Harrier CAP, which did not intercept us during the attack, jumped us from behind some minutes later during our egress along Falkland Sound. They immediately shot down myself and Lieutenant Márquez. Lieutenant Márquez got to Port Stanley (Puerto Argentino), guided by the nearby Fuerza Aérea mobile early warning radar; his aircraft, full of holes from 30mm gunfire, had both hydraulic control systems inoperative. Once over the airfield he tried to extend the landing gear but the left maingear had all but disappeared. He ejected over the bay beside the runway, being rescued sometime later by an Argentine army UH-1H helicopter.

Poor Lieutenant Márquez vanished without trace. Weeks later Arca told me that he had seen the ugly fireball and subsequent smoke cloud made by his Skyhawk after exploding. I remember quite frequently his anguished voice warning us of the Sea Harrier's presence. Gustavo was the Escuadrilla's youngest pilot; his sense of humour and dedication to duty had won him the full respect of his fellow officers. Personally he was the kind of wingman with whom I loved to fly.

When I ejected after the Sidewinder hit me, the A-4Q was flying at 500 knots, slightly nose high and at approximately 1,200ft. I had both helmet visors up due to the low visibility and showers we had encountered over Cape Meredith. I took the decision to eject when I saw a Sea Harrier close to me – perhaps for a second try – although my aircraft ought to have seemed doomed with the tail blown off. I do not remember if I put my head firmly back against the headrest, or if I slowed to less than 350 knots to avoid serious injury, as it is recommended in the NATPS manual. After pulling the seat pan handle I heard a loud bang as the canopy was blown off and the seat ejected. There was a sharp pain in my neck and my last thought before passing out was – 'I am breaking my neck' – like Lieutenant Peña (this pilot broke his neck after ejecting from his A-4Q A-216 on 16 January 1973). Regaining consciousness I found myself hanging from the parachute over Falkland Sound and drifting towards the shore of East Falkland (Is. Soledad), near King Bay …

The fact that my head was not resting on the back of the seat caused it to fall forward as I was propelled out of the seat, I felt a sharp pain in the back of my neck, my last thought before passing out was 'I'm falling apart like Lieutenant Peña' (a pilot of the Squadron who died as a result of a bad position during ejection). When I regained consciousness I found myself hanging from the parachute, over the water of the San Carlos Strait drifting towards the coast of Isla Soledad, towards the centre of Bahía Rey where the Navy transport *Río Carcarañá* was neutralized. I took off the helmet that was hanging from my forehead and that I don't know how it had slipped out of its normal place, given that I usually wear my mask and chinstrap tightly fastened. I looked for something to hook it to and when I couldn't find it I dropped it into space as I needed my hands free. Continuing with the established procedure practiced so many times in the Squadron's hang glider training, I inflated the waistcoat, unlocked the left adjuster and moved the seat pan (seat cushion attached to the pilot by a line and containing the raft and additional survival equipment) to the right, I looked for the dinghy hook and locked it into the harness eyebolt, then pulled the ring on the dinghy housing to unlock the dinghy, which revealed the inflation ring, which I proceeded to pull to inflate the dinghy. When I did not see any reaction, I took the CO_2 tube with my left hand, while with my right hand I repeated the manoeuvre, observing if the firing pin moved, but although everything was working normally, nothing happened. At this point the ground began to approach more rapidly, so I stopped worrying about the boat and concentrated on trying to determine the probable location of my landing. Within a few seconds I was able to determine the point in the sea where the parachute was heading, about 300m north of Cape Blanco. I tried to approach the shore by pulling on the canopy ropes, causing it to drift to the south, and almost immediately observed the parachute's reaction towards the shore. Close to touchdown I brought my hands to the release fittings of the sail and prepared my body for the impact, which was much harder than I thought it would be. Immediately after entering the water, the parachute canopy gently laid down and pulled me out of the water again, dragging me over the surface. When I saw that I was under control, that I could keep my head out of the water, and that it was taking me towards the coast, I gave up my attempts to detach myself from it, since, not having a dinghy, I wanted to get as close to the coast as possible, taking advantage of this unexpected help. At a certain point, the resistance offered by the seaweed (with the lifejacket inflated) and the dinghy and the seat pan increased and the wet canopy began to support me. I immediately and smoothly released the adjustments and started to swim towards the shore, but despite my efforts I noticed that I was not making any progress towards the shore, so I turned around and tried to swim backwards, with the same result. I started to check the dinghy again to try to inflate it, with the knife I hit the valve to try to unblock or defrost it, without obtaining any effect, I decided to disconnect the right fitting and the shackle that I had connected to the harness eyebolt during the parachute descent, with which I was totally free of this equipment, regretting having to abandon it and not being able to count on it to survive on land. While doing this I noticed that my legs and torso were entangled in seaweed, which I proceeded to cut off with the survival knife I carried in my waistcoat. Once I was free of everything that was preventing me from swimming, I started to swim backwards, now I was swimming towards the nearest shore, which was about 100m to the south. Twice I had to untangle myself from the seaweed until I finally managed to reach the shore. When I noticed that I was already standing I wanted to stand up and walk but I was so tired that I couldn't do it, and I had to get out of the water by helping myself with my hands. I was exhausted, my heart was beating so violently that I feared for a cardiac arrest. I tried to calm myself down, I looked at the clock, it was 3.30 pm. It was 30 minutes after the attack and 82 minutes after take-off. On two occasions, while I was resting, I heard and saw two Harriers flying low, following almost the same route we used on our approach to the target, first in a south-westerly direction, heading towards the southern mouth of the San Carlos Strait, and then in the opposite direction, returning to San Carlos. I was very worried about Lieutenant Rótolo's section coming 15 minutes behind me; I thought the British had intercepted them. I took out the Sarbe radio and listened several times on 282.8 with no result, then I made several calls to alert the planes, but nobody answered. At about 16.00 hours I got up and started to take off my waistcoat and harness. My back and right arm felt wet, so I spent some time drying my underwear and the Snow Wally I had on. I buried the harness in the sand and made my way to an elevation about 500m away, in order to get a better view of where I was and to get more antenna height for the emergency radio. For half an hour I kept the Sarbe broadcasting, while I looked for a separate place downwind to spend the night, as the sun would be setting in just over an hour. Every movement I made was accompanied by a sharp pain in the thigh of my left leg and at the base of my neck. in the middle of the Bahía del Rey was the *Río Carcarañá*. I spent several minutes watching it to try to discover signs of life but nothing was moving in its dead work, the anchor chain was taut and the ship was facing into the wind which indicated to me that it was floating well and that the crew had had time to leave it in an orderly fashion, the ship showed me the port side where no damage could be seen. In front of the bridge I saw something that I could not identify whether it was signs of a previous fire or natural deterioration due to rust. Looking at the waterline well out of the water I assumed that she would not have much in her holds either. I had hoped that at any moment I would see a boat lowered and come looking for me but nothing of the sort happened. I also looked towards the shores of the bay to try to see signs of her crew, but there was absolutely nothing. I found a ravine that assured me shelter from the wind and set about digging a shelter with the knife, piling stones and grass around what would be my bed for the night. I deflated the bladders of my lifejacket, except for one that would serve as a pillow, and arranged the rest so as to have as little contact as possible with the cold, wet ground. By the time I had finished it was already dark, the cold had gone out of me as a result of the movement and my clothes had dried. I wasn't hungry or thirsty, and even if I was, I wouldn't have eaten or drunk anything in the first 24 hours, as survival manuals advise. I tried to settle down as best I could to rest and only then could I think about everything that had happened, I thought about Graciela and the boys' worries, who would go to warn them, how would my numerals have fared, how would the battle in San Carlos be going? The sky was a shotgun of stars, the clouds that had been there during the afternoon had dissipated and visibility was excellent, I was feeling better despite the pain in my leg and neck; I wasn't worried about being alone, it was a familiar experience during the stalking of wild boar hogs. I knew that after three o'clock in the morning the cold would not be bearable and I was prepared for that too. With all these thoughts I became drowsy. When I was very cold I would sit up, switch on the Sarbe and leave it emitting on a rock while I warmed up by deepening my foxhole. When I got warm again, I would switch off the Sarbe and lie down again. I was half asleep when I was startled by a great brightness in the sky coming from flares falling softly over the *Río Carcarañá*; almost simultaneously loud explosions were heard in the superstructure of the ship and in its vicinity. From a frigate, which I could not see, artillery fire was being directed at the neutralized merchantman. I thought that the landing in San Carlos was accompanied by others in different parts of the island and this was one of them, so I grabbed my survival waistcoat, made sure I had my knife, pistol and radio and started walking south. It was 02:30. I walked until dawn, when it was light enough I went to the highest elevation of the land, so I could see better towards King's Bay. There I could see the poor *Río Carcarañá* heeling over and sending up a dense column of smoke that could be seen from far away. I took out the Sarbe, checked the battery status, plugged it in and left it on a rock, emitting its signal. I found a place to lie down to eat my breakfast of survival candy and a few sips of water, then cracked open a piece of gum. A pair of Harriers circled over San Carlos, then began a north-south dive, to what I estimated to be Darwin, without descending much, perhaps 10,000ft, turned left and climbed again, tracking. They moved off in a north-

> easterly direction. It was 07:00 on 22 May. At that time it was 24 hours since my last formal meal, breakfast. I looked around trying to locate any houses or villages but there was nothing to be seen. I switched off the Sarbe, settled my equipment and started walking south. I knew from the mapping of the island that there were ranch posts in the area, and on the approach to the target I saw a group of fuel drums on the beach and where there is fuel there are people nearby. I walked all day, eating a piece of candy and a sip of water every four hours. Chewing gum helped to keep my mouth moist and to trick my stomach, and at dusk that day I arrived at an abandoned shearing shed, practically dragging my left leg. When I was about 200m from it, I sat down to rest, while observing the place to check for the presence of other people. About half an hour later, without seeing any signs of life, I approached the place, it was about 16:00 and it would soon get dark so I started to inspect the place looking for food and combustible elements to light a fire, I didn't want to spend another night like the previous one. Inside the shed there was no food but there was plenty of wood, some beds and a table, probably for the use of the staff who came to work during the shearing season. Walking around the outside I found a store of peat with which I immediately set about preparing a fire. According to the basic rules, with the knife I made several small splinters, then larger ones, and so on, until I finally piled up several pieces of dry peat. I dumped the contents of the survival waistcoat on the table and proceeded to arrange and count what I had …

On 24 May 1982 Philippi was found by Tony Blake, manager of a sheep ranch and with great kindness he took him to his house, where he introduced him to his family and provided him with everything he needed – food, bath, bed and above all radio contact with the command of the Argentine forces in Port Stanley. The next day an Air Force Bell 212 took him to Darwin and on the 26th a CH-47C Chinook took him to Port Stanley, where he spent the night; the following day, just at midnight, he would be evacuated to Río Gallegos in a C-130H Hercules, and finally, on 29 May, a Skyvan of the Prefectura Naval took him to Río Grande, where he was reunited with his family and comrades.

ARA *25 de Mayo* operating during the crisis with Chile, with eleven A-4Q Skyhawks, four S-2E Trackers and three S-61D Sea Kings.

An A-4Q armed with AIM-9B Sidewinder missiles during the southern deployment in December 1978. At that time, unsuccessful attempts were made to purchase more modern versions of the Sidewinder, such as the AIM-9E or AIM-9J.

A-4Q 3-A-308 taxiying to the bow capapult.

3-A-304 using the Sargent Fletcher Buddy Pack for in-flight refuelling 3-A-309.

3-A-305 preparing to be catapulted from *25 de Mayo* in the late 1970s.

A-4Q aircraft armed with bombs and rockets aboard the aircraft carrier. Behind, four destroyers of the Argentine Navy.

Aircraft 3-A-307 and 314 were two of the three A-4Qs lost in combat on 21 May 1982 after attacking HMS *Ardent*.

Taxiing to the catapult.

Lieutenant Commander Jorge Philippi, leader of the ill-fated 'Tábano' flight.

HMS *Ardent* damaged and on fire in the waters of San Carlos, after the 'visit' by 'Tábano' flight.

Chapter 8

One-Way Mission, Part II

Lieutenant José César Arca was one of the two wingmen in the unfortunate 'Tábano' division, and in the following lines narrates his dramatic ordeal of being shot down and trying to survive.

At the start of the attack run narrated by the formation leader (Philippi) and going into the target as number two, my distance from Lieutenant Commander Philippi's Skyhawk was not the briefed 19 seconds to avoid the debris of his bombs, it was only some seven/ten seconds, I did not try to open up to get the correct one, as during the hard turn towards the frigate a real curtain of anti-aircraft fire was between both of us and the ship. The run-in towards the target was at very low altitude, the splashes and explosions on the water were too near the jets for comfort. I clearly remember during that bombing run, how a missile was fired from the ship, then I turned hard right trying to avoid it, then returning to the original heading to continue with the attack. Due to the small difference in time with the leader, the procedures for aiming were almost simultaneous, I saw as Lieutenant Commander Philippi's four bombs dropped out from the centreline rack and how their Snakeye tails opened up, to establish the pre-established sequence. Up until that time I hoped he could miss in order I did not have debris problems, but the fourth bomb made a direct hit on the stern, provoking a violent explosion, and I had no alternative, at the same time as the leader said on the radio, 'One on the stern', to launching my bombs, then flying through the column of fire and smoke, after leaving behind this hellish image, Lieutenant Márquez said, 'Another hit on the stern'.

Now on the escape stage, flying parallel to left shore of the Estrecho de San Carlos (Falkland Sound) heading south/southwest (which was the right side during our approach to the target), I got visual contact with the leader at some 1,000m to my left while Lieutenant Márquez was some 1,000–1,500m to my right side. Just 15 seconds after having positively identified both, Lieutenant Márquez's anguished voice over the radio almost stopped my heart: 'Sea Harriers, there'. At that moment I turned my head towards the leader and saw a Sidewinder leaving the launch rail of a Sea Harrier behind him, after a short flight the missile flew up the tailpipe of Philippi's Skyhawk, then I turn my head to the right, I did not see Márquez's jet, although a Sea Harrier was behind and to the right. Almost simultaneously the first 30mm gunfire burst hits me on the right wing, as I was flying very close to the water, some 10ft above it, the skidding caused by the hits almost made me crash into it, I barely controlled the jet, and my only thought was to turn into my pursuer in order to break his gunnery solution, but then I was hit by another burst. Quickly I made the ejection procedures, as I had a total hydraulic failure, without oxygen and almost losing all electrical power. I switched to manual control at 480 knots, as the controls had turned very hard, in spite that NATOPS says that the maximum speed for switching to manual is 250 knots, while I turned into one of the Sea Harriers.

The combat with the Sea Harriers lasted for about 40 to 60 seconds. I do not know why they left me without completing the kill, perhaps they were short on fuel or they had spent all their weapons. Then I headed towards Puerto Argentino following the coastline, trying to avoid Goose Green, I was flying with manual controls, at low altitude and with 500 knots in the clock, while the fuel indicator showed 1,100lbs remaining, but diminishing, as I was losing it at an alarming rate through the 30mm shell holes in the wings, six on the right and four on the left. My next worry was to avoid colliding with the ground due to the conditions that I flew and contact with the controlling people at Puerto Argentino to avoid being shot at by the air defences.

After trying many times to raise them on the radio, I made contact with a helicopter which was flying near the area and asked him to relay my message to the Combat Operations Centre, then by the same channel I did hear a radio message in English between two Sea Harriers, and decided to cease using the radio for fear of being located. I continued flying and with the help of a map I found Fitz Roy settlement, I was near, thus I called them again on the radio telling me: 'We have you on the radar, eject!'. For me it did not seem a good idea and replied in the negative, as my intention was to arrive with the Skyhawk over the airfield, and the controller agreed with me. Now they had me on visual contact. But I could not discern the airfield's runway, thus I received instructions for the approach. I proceeded to lower the landing gear, appearing two greens, for the nose and right main gear, while the left one was not secured. I informed about it and requested a low pass over the tower to check it out. Once I did it, Brigadier Iarannello, the tower controller, said 'Look, you haven´t any landing gear on the left, I can see the sky through the many holes you have on the wings, go and eject over the bay.'

I did not have any other possibility, my intention was to land and save my faithful 3-A-312, so I climbed to 2,500ft heading to the ejection area which he said. I completely removed the oxygen mask from the helmet and I pulled the overhead ejection handle. This is a very difficult moment for a fast jet pilot, as there is always the feeling of the unknown after the ejection, but one acts almost in automatic gear.

After a violent explosion and having the feeling of somersaulting I was hanging from the parachute and in complete silence. The Skyhawk did not want to part me, as after making a slight descending turn, came head on to me, perhaps trying to ram me due to my abandoning it, but it continued its descending turns, for a couple of times, until due to the danger it represented, the AAA opened fire and shot it down.

Simultaneously with this half-dramatic half-funny situation, I fulfilled the procedure of inflating the life vest, removing my gloves, and as I was very near the water, I did not pull the dinghy out of the survival pack, getting ready to unfasten the fittings at

> the moment of contacting with the sea. Now on the water, not very comfortable due to the weight of the pack and the dinghy which I had not removed, I saw an Army UH-1H helicopter hovering near me ready to rescue me. But this machine was in the 'slick' configuration with door machine guns, not having any type of rescue gear, thus the gunner lowered a rope, which broke twice due to excessive weight. Several times the helicopter put its skis in the water, even touching my head twice with its belly. It was infuriating to be physically so near but far due to its lack of rescue means. During 20 minutes we fought trying to get me inside the helicopter, but as all attempts were in vain and as I was starting to feel freezing symptoms on the feet and hands, I signalled the helicopter to get out in order to think about the situation. The shore was at about 500m, and I decided to remove part of the survival kit, including the life vest and started swimming towards the beach, still with the heavy flight boots and the anti-exposure suit. When only 200m remained they advised that I could not go as the beach was mined! Thus I had not any other alternative, but to try again to climb into the helicopter. By hand signals I called it, as it was hovering near me. I knew that this would be one of my last opportunities to survive, thus when it approached and sank the skis in the water, I got one of them with hands and feet, like riding it but from its lower side, I shouted to the gunner, who with his body hanging out grabbed my head and neck: 'Now or never'. Automatically the pilot headed to the shore and in a safe place, while hovering at about 3ft, I fell hard onto the rocky ground. Then the helicopter landed and I was helped inside, bringing me to the hospital. During the short hop, tiredness, both physical and mental got hold, my eyes tried to close, to which the gunner tried to avoid slapping my face with his hand. Within minutes I was in the hospital and got the treatment according to my state. My right arm was plastered, and two days later, I was again fit and before the month's end I returned in a cargo plane to the mainland.

Moments after the attack of the first division, the second arrived at the San Carlos Strait, the TN Roberto Sylvester relates

> The mission was to attack a damaged ship at the western mouth of the San Carlos channel [possibly it was the ELMA *Río Carcarañá*, sighted by FAA planes and confused with a British ship – Author] and if not found, advance through the strait to San Carlos Bay, attacking the first enemy ship to be sighted. The navigation was exact and we stopped at the point provided in the grazing flight. We turned to starboard and headed for Aguila Island to verify the presence of the likely damaged ship at the mouth of the strait. We listened to the ejection communication from the leader of the first section and immediately tried to communicate with the numerals, to no avail. We closed the column formation in order to allow flexibility to the leader and not lose sight of ourselves and we ended up in the Bay of Ruiz Puente. There were four ships, the leader assigned the closest one and we started the approach to attack it. We do it at low altitude, high speed completing our mission uneventfully, contrary to what happened to the first division.

Skyhawk 3-A-301 armed with ten 125kg Mk 81 bombs. The internal forward position of the Multiple Ejector Rack was not used because the bombs could hit the landing gear covers.

Lieutenant Julio César Arca.

Remains of A-4Q 3-A-312 after the ejection of Lieutenant Arca off Puerto Argentino on 21 May 1982.

HMS *Ardent* being helped by the frigate HMS *Plymouth*.

Left: A pair of Sea Harrier FRS1s landing aboard HMS *Invincible* after an uneventful CAP.

Below: Close-up of an 800 NAS Sea Harrier with three 'kill' marks; the Argentine dubbed it 'La Muerte Negra' ('The Black Death')

HMS *Plymouth* alongside the ill-fated HMS *Ardent*.

Chapter 9

Tercera Escuadrilla Aeronaval de Caza y Ataque Casualties

A-4Q 0660/3-A-307

21 May 1982. At 15:05 after attacking the frigate HMS *Ardent*, scoring one hit, 307 was jumped by Sea Harrier FRS.1 XZ457 from 800 NAS flown by Lieutenant Morrell and shot down by an AIM-9L which flew up the Skyhawk's tailpipe, blowing off the entire tail area. Its pilot, Lieutenant Commander Alberto Jorge Philippi, ejected, returning to Río Grande on 30 May 1982. The Skyhawk crashed into the water, near the southern mouth of Falkland Sound.

A-4Q 0667/3-A-314

21 May 1982. At 15:05 after attacking the frigate HMS *Ardent*, without scoring any hits, 314 was jumped by Sea Harrier FRS.1XZ500 from 800 NAS flown by Flight Lieutenant Leeming. Being too close to use a Sidewinder, Leeming delivered a long burst of 30mm Aden cannon fire into the A-4Q. Most of the heavy shells found their mark and the Skyhawk disintegrated into a violent explosion. The pilot, Sub Lieutenant Gustavo Marcelo Márquez was killed instantly and wreckage fell into the Sound.

A-4Q 0665/3-A-312

21 May 1982. At 15:20 after attacking the frigate HMS *Ardent*, scoring one hit, 312 was jumped by Lieutenant Morrell (after shooting down 307). An AIM-9L was launched, but did not guide well. Morrell followed up with guns, getting at least ten hits. Lieutenant Jose Cesar Arca tried to land at Port Stanley, but was prevented by damage to his landing gear. After bailing out he was rescued by an Army helicopter. The Skyhawk continued flying and had to be shot down by Argentine AA fire, crashing on the shore, some 500m south of the airfield.

A-4Q 0659/3-A-306

23 May 1982. At 15:15 while attacking the frigate HMS *Antelope* Lieutenant Commander Carlos Zubizarreta suffered an electrical failure and his bombs failed to release. Rather than jettison the bombs and Multiple Ejector Rack he elected to return to Río Grande

to save them for another mission. After touchdown on the wet and icy runway with such a heavy load, he failed to engage the emergency arresting gear.

Veering off the runway, Zubizarreta thought that without control his A-4Q and with the possibility of the bombs detonating, it was better to eject. Unfortunately the rocket booster was time expired and did not propel the pilot high enough. He landed heavily on the runway with a partially deployed parachute and died soon afterwards in hospital. Damage to the A-4Q was light and it was repaired and returned to active service, but six months later, on 11 November, while on a night sortie from Comandante Espora Naval Air Station, 306 crashed near the airfield, killing its young pilot, Ensign Loubet Jambert.

Tercera Escuadrilla groundcrews seen at Río Grande during the war. In the background two camouflaged A-4Qs can be seen.

3-A-301 and an unidentified A-4Q in Río Grande during the last days of the war. After the three losses to Sea Harriers on 21 May, it was decided to camouflage the jets, to make their detection more difficult.

3-A-304 was one of the A-4Qs that received green and brown shades during the war, as did 3-A-301, 302, 305, and 306. 3-A-309 received a different scheme.

By 1984 the A-4Qs received a new paint scheme, with bluish gray on the top, and bottom in light gray. This scheme was similar to that adopted by the Tracker, Sea King, EMB-326 Xavante and other naval aviation aircraft.

3-A-304 reverted to its original scheme after the war.

This is a former US Navy A-4B, owned by a civilian warbird collector in the US who has restored and painted it as A-4Q 3-A-305.

Chapter 10

After the War

During June 1982, Tercera Escuadrilla Aeronaval de Caza y Ataque returned to Comandante Espora Naval Air Station and was awarded the Honor for courage in combat distinction. On 15 and 16 October, the Squadron embarked again on the aircraft carrier, operating alongside the Super Étendard, and during that year the activity was intense, with six aircraft assigned, four of which had new wings, although it was decided that 3-A-302, due to its condition, would not operate on board again.

Between 25 and 28 October 1982, aircraft 3-A-304, 306, 308 and 309 embarked on the aircraft carrier for the Fraterno IV operation with the Brazilian Navy, carrying out several sorties. Ensign Loubet Jambert died in a night accident in November 1982 during a training flight near Espora at the controls of 3-A-306. This was the first and only time that the same Argentine single-seater combat aircraft claimed the lives of two pilots (Lieutenant Commander Zubizarreta and Ensign Loubet) on two separate occasions.

At that time, the installation of 30mm cannon, Librascope HUDs, radio altimeter, TACAN Hoffman AN/ARN-91 and VLF Omega Series II were re-evaluated, although these changes were not made. During 1983 combat exercises of different performance were carried out against the Super Étendard and in 1984 the unit received a low availability of aircraft due to wear of the material and the squadron continued with only three machines being used for training. That year the planes received chaff launchers and flares, and a digital intervalometer was tested on 3-A-304. In addition, the change to the paint scheme was started with one in dark gray above and light gray below, which was first applied in 3-A-302.

During May 1982 and in the midst of the war, as part of the urgent re-equipment negotiated by the Argentine government to replace the losses of the war, the purchase of twelve Israeli A-4E aircraft was processed to replace the machines lost in the war. Israel authorized the sale of them and, as the war ended before the purchase was finalized, it was decided to modernize them with a navigation and attack platform developed by Elbit Systems, called LCWDNS (Low Cost Weapons Delivery and Navigation System) with a digital INS and HUD. Work began in late 1984, and the planes were expected to arrive in the country in 1985 for local modification, with six of them entering service in 1986. The planes were registered 3-A-301 to 312 and two of them received the paint scheme in shades of gray that had just been applied to the A-4Qs.

However, because the export of the aircraft had to be authorized by the United States, the delivery could not be made, despite the fact that Argentina had already made 80 per cent of the payment. The United States did not authorize the sale, and the aircraft were held in Israel. Negotiations continued, studying the installation of the new equipment in the A-4Qs, which was not possible without major structural modifications, and finally an agreement was reached by which the operation was undone and with the money paid, the S-2E Tracker and some spare parts for the A-4Qs and three Sargent Fletcher refuelling pods were purchased.

On 22 May 1986, the last accident of the naval Skyhawk took place, when 3-A-305 lost power when making a touch and go at the Comandante Espora Naval Air Station and the pilot, Lieutenant José Plá, ejected.

On 19 July 1986, onboard activities ended and Lieutenant Médici had the honour of performing the final catapult launch of an A-4Q with 3-A-301, after 15 intense years of operations. At that time only 3-A-302 / -304 / -309 were available.

Then 3-A-304 was decommissioned and with the remaining two aircraft the 3rd Squadron became dependent on the 2nd Naval Fighter and Attack Squadron. At that time it was studied to extend their life and use them for resupply missions, reconnaissance, electronic warfare and training. However, the lack of funds prevented this from taking place.

The last aircraft in service was 3-A-302, which had received the wing of 3-A-308 and was used for test flights of electronic equipment. The deactivation of the unit occurred on 25 February 1988, during a ceremony in Espora; the final training of the personnel being carried out together with the last Skyhawk of Naval Aviation. After said event, Lieutenant Médici at the controls of 3-A-302 made the final flight to the Jorge Newbery Airport in Buenos Aires, escorted by two Super Étendard, a Beech T-34C. Turbo Mentor and an EMB-326GB Xavante. After landing, the A-4 was transferred to the Army Mechanics School (ESMA) to be used as educational material. Today the aircraft is exhibited in the Comandante Espora Naval Museum.

A-4Q Skyhawk carrier operations

Year	Catapult launches	Carrier traps
1974	177*	177*
1975	471*	795*
1976	172*	172*
1977	145	141
1978	–	–
1979	230	218
1980	263	263
1981	203	204
1982	108	110
1983	83	87
1984	37	37
1985	249**	249**
1986	132**	132

* Shared with S-2E Tracker and T-28P Fennec aircraft.
** Shared with S-2E Tracker and AMD/BA Super Étendard aircraft.

Sylvester, Rótolo and Lecour (from left to right in that order) in mid-2006, and then second Chief of Staff of the Argentine Navy Rótolo. His two numerals were already retired from active duty.

3-A-304 (forward) and 305 in Río Grande after having been camouflaged during the war. You can see the difference in tones on the planes. Behind are an Aermacchi MB-326 and two 339s.

3-A-302 in July, 1986, catching the wire, the pilot Lieutenant Federico Larrinaga.

3-A-304 during operations aboard the *25 de Mayo* in October 1982 for the Fraternal IV exercise, with the Brazilian Navy. In the photo it was piloted by Lieutenant Commander Castro Fox.

Last flight of the A-4Q in Argentina, with 3-A-302 escorted by the Super Étendard 3-A-214 bound for Buenos Aires.

Two of the A-4Es destined for the Argentine Navy. The one behind shows the Argentine paint scheme, although without the national markings.

When Brazil decided to purchase the A-4KU, the aircraft carrier NAeL *Minas Gerais* moved to the Puerto Belgrano Naval Base, where it embarked A-4Q 3-A-302, at that time already at the Museo de Naval Aviation, to test the handling of the Skyhawk on the deck and the ship's hangar.

Some of the A-4Es destined for Argentina as they were still stored in Hatzerim, Israel, in 2008.

This is a former US Navy A-4B, owned by a civilian warbird collector in the US who has restored and painted it as A-4Q 3-A-305.

Chapter 11

After the War, the Argentine Air Force Fightinghawks

In the early 1990s, the Argentine Air Force began to seriously consider a replacement for the Skyhawk, with particular interest in the F/A-18 Hornet and the F-16 Fighting Falcon.

The United States' refusal to deliver this material was categorical and, in return, it authorized the sale of a batch of fifty-four Skyhawks, of which forty-eight would be single-seat A-4Ms and six two-seat OA-4Ms (the only aircraft model approved by the US Congress to be delivered to the Argentine Air Force). Given the antiquated nature of their electronic systems, the FAA requested their modernisation with more sophisticated technology. The authorization of the sale of this material implied a virtual lifting of the US arms embargo imposed after the Falklands War. The plan then developed by the FAA was to operate the aircraft for ten years, while the purchase of F-16s or similar aircraft was negotiated. Logistical support was negotiated for that period of time.

Immediately, the Ministry of Defence and the FAA began to hear bids from different companies for the upgrade contract. Among them was the American company Smith Industries, which partnered with the US Navy and offered an interesting upgrade programme. At the same time, in October 1992, McDonnell Douglas and the Spanish company CASA presented a project for the refurbishment of the aircraft in Spain. The package included, in turn, the renewal of the avionics of the Mirage IIIs in service with the VI Air Brigade. All this work was to be financed by credits provided by the Spanish government. This alternative did not prosper, and in March 1994 McDonnell Douglas made a new offer, this time for twenty-three Kuwaiti A-4KUs repowered by this company, which was also unsuccessful, as their condition was not what the Argentinians wanted. Four years later, the same A-4KUs were acquired by the Marinha Brasileira. The FAA was inclined to accept Smith Industries' offer and signed a pre-contract. By then, it had already acquired thirty-two A-4Ms and four OA-4Ms from the US Navy for a total price of $70 million.

Almost at the same time, in March 1994, the Argentine Ministry of Defence accepted Lockheed Aircraft's proposal to take over the concession of the Military Aircraft Factory (FMA) in the city of Cordoba, and the modernisation of the A-4, partly in the United States and partly in Argentina. In this way, the pre-contract with Smith was scrapped. The awarding of the privatized FMA was a determining factor in the negotiations with Lockheed. Thus Lockheed Aircraft Argentina S.A. (LAASA) was created in the facilities of the now defunct FMA. For an amount of $214 million, the reconditioning and upgrading of the thirty-six Skyhawks was stipulated, eighteen of which would be carried out in Cordoba and the rest in Lockheed's plant in Ontario (United States). The entire programme was named the A-4AR Fightinghawk Project and Commodore Horacio Mir Gonzalez was appointed Head of the programme. He immediately ordered the transfer of personnel from Technical Group 5, under the command of Vice Commodore Oscar G. Sanchez, to the AMARC (Aircraft Maintenance And Regeneration Center) at Davis-Monthan AFB (Arizona) to carry out an exhaustive inspection of the pre-selected machines.

A key part of the contract was the supply of the Westinghouse APG-66 radar that equipped the F-16A. The decision by the US Congress to authorize the sale of this, by then, powerful radar led to unsuccessful protests and pressure from the British government to stop the deal. Selected Skyhawks began to be flown from AMARC to Ontario to begin work and the first Skyhawk flew in on 2 August 1995. This machine, registered C-905 and christened 'Gaucho 02', along with C-906 'Gaucho 01' were the first to fly in the United States with Argentine registration. At the same time, the facilities in Cordoba were being prepared to receive the aircraft that would be modernized there.

On 30 September of that year, the first four units arrived in Cordoba, and in successive shipments the remaining units were received, bringing the total to twenty-seven, nine more aircraft than originally planned, thus reducing the number to be modernized in the United States. The contract also provided for the delivery of several batches of various A-4 models to be used as spare parts, including six A-4Fs, four A-4Ms, one OA-4M and two TA-4Js. These were taken to the Río IV Material Area (ARMACUAR) and to the plant of the now Lockheed Martin Aircraft Argentina (LMAASA), both in the province of Córdoba. Technical Group 5 received sixteen training simulators for the different systems that make up the aircraft. This allowed the specialists to quickly adapt to the new aircraft.

A-4ARs arrive in Argentina

The Fightinghawk modernisation programme included replacing the tail section of the OA-4AMs with an A-4M tail section, which has parachute brakes. The engine of the A-4AR and OA-4AR remains the same as the A-4M and OA-4M, a Pratt & Whitney J-52-P-408A, with 11,200lbs thrust in the former and a J-52-P8A with 9,300lbs thrust in the two-seater. In addition, the latter underwent some modifications such as the Out Ship Blast (OSB) failure control system. The A-4AR also has an autonomous start-up system, so it does not need ground support, which is not provided on the two-seaters. Despite having inferior performance to the single-seater, the A-4AR can be used as a complement for certain types of missions and could be fitted with a laser designator operable from the rear position (as used by the Chilean Air Force on its Mirage Elkan tandem-seat aircraft), making it a target marker for bombs guided by the aforementioned means. The options are varied, which made the OA-4AR a system with a very important potential, not only for pilot training and reconnaissance, although in the end this capability was not used.

The main part of the avionics is the ARG-1 radar, which is a version, with a reduced antenna for space reasons, of the APG-66 used on the F-16 Fighting Falcon, capable of detecting aircraft at a distance of 100km in air-to-air mode, 40km in air-to-surface and

100km in mapping mode. Through software enhancements, its capability was taken from just the equivalent of an F-16 Block 15 to the equivalent of a Block 40. To mount the radar, the nose section of the OA/A-4M received structural changes and a new nose cone was designed using composite material similar to that employed on the F-117 Nighthawk. The radar software supports the use of smart weaponry such as laser-guided bombs, and AGM-65 Maverick and AIM-9M Sidewinder missiles, among others from a variety of sources. It is linked to the cockpit by two LCD Multifunction Head Down Displays (HDD), an Up Front Control Panel (UFCP) and a Smart Head Up Display (SHUD). In addition, the Fightinghawk has HOTAS (Hands on Throttle and Stick) controls. The original joystick controls were removed and replaced by a new joystick and gas control with a large number of buttons that move the cursors on the two display screens without removing the hands from the flight controls.

It also has an AN/ARL-93 (V-1) Radar Warning Receiver (RWR), two EGI-2 laser inertial platforms with GPS, IFF, chaff and flare launcher, MADC air data computer and an air data transducer (ADT). They have a digital mission computer, with a ground mission mapping system, where mission information is entered by the pilot and then fed into the aircraft using a Data Transfer Module (DTM). Above the engine compartment the Fightinghawk has the VHF equipment and avionics cooling system and the aircraft also has an autonomous on-board oxygen generation system.

Other innovations include an integrated electronic countermeasures system and a radar jamming system. Many of the crews received specialized electronic warfare training on the FAA's VR-21-registered Boeing 707-387C, which was upgraded by IAI for electronic warfare and electronic intelligence missions. All avionics are connected by fibre optics which enhances centralized data control. It also contains a 16-bit MIL-STD-1553B data link, which connects to a laptop via fibre optics, making avionics maintenance less complicated.

Along with the aircraft, a fully digitized flight simulator was delivered, with liquid crystal displays that allow a 180° view. The software has graphics of all the surroundings of the V Air Brigade. It is an A-4M simulator that was brought to the standard of Argentine aircraft by the North American company Camber Corporation. After being qualified and checked for perfect operation in Palmdale, it was disassembled and taken to the V Air Brigade. This vital instrument was intensively used by the first A-4AR pilots who received instruction at Lockheed Martin before making the ferry flights that brought the aircraft into the country.

The current C-906 is not the original 'Gaucho 01', as this first aircraft was found to have structural deficiencies which meant that it was never converted into an A-4AR. Thus, there were thirty-seven machines that bore the Argentine registration number. Currently the front part of this airframe (Bu. Nu. 158417) is in the museum of the V Air Brigade.

After more than two years of work, the first five fighter-bombers were delivered at a major ceremony on 12 December 1997 at Lockheed Martin Skunk Works in Palmdale. These were four A-4ARs (registration numbers C-906, -908, -917 and -918) and one OA-4AR (C-903) which began the long journey to Argentina on the same day. The first ferry stop was at Davis Monthan AFB where the five aircraft were manned by Lockheed

Martin pilots. There, the formal transfer of the aircraft was signed, continuing the journey the next day with stops at Monterrey and Ixtepec airports (Mexico) and Howard AFB (Panama). On the 16th they departed for Chiclayo and Pisco (Peru) and on the 17th from there to Viru-Viru airport in Santa Cruz de la Sierra (Bolivia). On the morning of the 18th, they flew the final leg, touching down on Argentine soil at 13:15 on the runway of the 1st Air Brigade at El Palomar (Buenos Aires Province).

Five days later, the new weapon system was officially presented to the President of the Nation, Carlos Menem, and that same day they left for their final destination. C-903, commanded by Vice Commodore Juan Alberto Macaya, was the first Fightinghawk to land over Reynolds.

The new machines began to integrate Squadrons I and II of Fighter Group 5, passing to Squadron III the A-4Bs and Cs that were still in service. At the end of 1997, Commodore Mir Gonzalez assumed command of the V Air Brigade and Commodore Jorge D. Senn took charge of the A-4AR Project to begin the comprehensive harmonisation phase of the programme for the aircraft's sophisticated systems. With the completion of the modernisation of three Fightinghawks in the United States, the second ferry began. In late May 1998, A-4AR C-907 and OA-4AR C-902 and C-904 departed for V Air Brigade, where they arrived on 4 June. During this ferry they were scheduled to stop in Tegucigalpa, Honduras, but the airport had to be closed due to bad weather and only La Aurora airport in Guatemala City remained open in the area. Diplomatic efforts had to be made against the clock to get the Guatemalan government to authorize the landing of the Argentinian fighter planes while they were on standby. Finally, permission was granted and the three planes made a stopover at the airport.

On 3 August, the first modernized A-4AR (C-922) was delivered to LMAASA. Successive deliveries continued until 7 January 2000, when the last two aircraft (C-905 and C-916) were delivered. Due to the lack of pilots, it was never possible to operate all the machines at the same time, so some were preserved shortly after arrival. Over time, the machines were rotated, which allowed the originally planned service time of ten years to be far exceeded, reaching twenty years in 2017. However, this was done at the cost of maintaining a very low level of operability, to which the ever-increasing budget cuts experienced in the new millennium contributed greatly.

Homologation of weapon systems and retrofit plan

On 1 October 1998, the A-4AR C-906 was flown to the United States by sea, where it joined the OA-4AR C-901 that was still at the Lockheed Martin plant to begin the homologation flights of the weapons and navigation systems, giving way to the second stage of the A-4AR Project. For this purpose, Major Eduardo La Torre was sent to carry out these tests together with Lockheed's test pilots. In early 1999, Captain Claudio Trerótola was commissioned to Singapore to evaluate the BVR EHUD combat training pod, of Israeli origin, used by the local Air Force on its A-4s and manufactured by BVR Technologies Ltd. The system's satisfactory performance led to its subsequent acquisition.

During their stay in the United States, the aircraft were intensively test flown with a wide variety of weapons and configurations in order to achieve perfect coordination and interaction of all systems in the different combat modes (air-to-air, air-to-surface and air-to-sea). The AIM-9L Sidewinder inert missile began to be used alongside the EHUD, testing the behaviour of the avionics, especially the ARG-1 radar and the mission computer. During homologation, successive modifications and upgrades were made to the electronic equipment. Starting with Block A, the avionics with which the first eight aircraft were delivered from the United States, Block B, C, C1, C2, C3, C3A and C3B were passed through until reaching the final Block C software and hardware Block C version C3Bn, receiving 130 modifications since its entry into service, so that the original SDLM (Standard Depot Level Maintenance) had to be redesigned, since the old parameters could not be met due to the permanent upgrade to which this weapon system is subjected. This version represented the maximum capability of the A-4AR equipment. In January 2000, work was completed in the United States and the aircraft were shipped to Argentina. They arrived at the port of Buenos Aires on 10 February and after being reassembled at Austral's facilities in Aeroparque, they left for Villa Reynolds on 21 February.

In order to standardize the entire A-4AR fleet to the final block, an agreement was signed with LMAASA to execute the retrofit plans. These were carried out at the Cordoba plant, at ARMACUAR and at Technical Group 5. In this way, the OA/A-4AR weapon system reached an optimum level of operability.

At that time, an offer was received from the US government for twenty-three TA-4J Skyhawks, with the aim of using them for the FAA's fighter school and retiring the FMA IA-63 Pampa. The poor condition of the aircraft offered and the FAA's interest in keeping the Pampa aircraft operational, despite the problems in obtaining spare parts, led to the proposal being discarded and the FAA preferring to negotiate with LMAASA for the provision of spare parts for the trainers.

Training

In January 2000, four Lockheed instructor pilots arrived at the V Air Brigade to give a course on the tactical operation of the A-4AR Block C3Bn. The course lasted seven months, during which the Argentine pilots received a total of 40 hours of theoretical instruction, 190 hours in a flight simulator, 200 hours of air-to-ground combat and 350 hours of air-to-air combat. The training flights were divided into three stages: navigation, air-to-ground combat and air-to-air combat. For the last two stages, the EHUD was used intensively and proved to be an excellent training aircraft. From March, the inert AIM-9L training missile began to be used in close conjunction with the EHUD. In the meantime, the AIM-9M Sidewinder warfare missiles were awaited.

The EHUD ACMI (Air Combat Maneuvering Instrumentation) was a training system for air-to-air, air-to-surface and electronic warfare missions. It is installed in the body of an AIM-9L Sidewinder training missile and can be easily retrofitted to the aircraft. On a training sortie, the participating aircraft (carrying the EHUD) are interconnected with each other and the command post in the brigade. In this way it was possible to follow the mission alternatives in real time. Once on the ground, the pilots could debrief the mission using the parameters recorded by the EHUD. It made it possible to recreate a real virtual polygon where it was possible to simulate air or ground collisions, rule violations and border crossings. It made it possible to simulate the firing of guns and missiles and to evaluate hits or shoot-downs, taking into account the manoeuvres of the opponent and the electronic countermeasures employed. In air-to-ground mode, it had ballistics tables that allowed the trajectory of bombs to be simulated in order to establish the point of impact in relation to the target. It could also simulate dynamic threats such as anti-aircraft missile sites and interact with the aircraft's radar warning receiver (RWR). Due to budget constraints, this system was withdrawn from service in the second decade of the new millennium when it was decommissioned and spare parts could not be purchased.

Maintenance includes hourly, cyclic and/or component condition inspections. Basically, they can be divided into three types: 'O' (Operational), performed without the need for infrastructure; 'I' (Intermediate), which due to their complexity, must be performed in a hangar; and 'D' (Depot) – 50 hours or 39 months – must be performed in the Río IV Material Area and covers all A-4AR electronics maintenance, as well as everything related to structural overhauls.

Exercises

In March 1998 the Fightinghawk made its first international appearance when an A-4AR flew across the Andes to participate in FIDAE 98 at Los Cerrillos airport in Santiago, Chile. The first exercise in which the Fightinghawk participated was 'Antuna I' on 26 June 1998. It consisted of an air-to-ground firing and air defence demonstration carried out at the Antuna Firing Range, where Finger fighter-bombers and Canberra bombers of the VI and II Air Brigade respectively also participated and was the first opportunity for the A-4ARs to use live ammunition.

In August of that year, the joint exercise Aguila I was carried out between different FAA units and F-16C/D Fighting Falcon Block 30 aircraft from the Alabama Air National Guard, USA. The exercise took place at the V Air Brigade, in which Mirage IIIEA, Finger (both from the VI Air Brigade), OA/A-4AR and F-16 aircraft conducted air-to-air tactical exercises. Through Aguila I, the FAA had the opportunity to obtain important information on the performance of its front-line combat aircraft and to strengthen ties with the United States in this type of exercise, which resulted in an invaluable exchange of knowledge and experience.

In the autumn and spring of 1999, the Argentine Patagonia was the destination of the first deployments of the Fightinghawk Squadron. The first of these took place at the IX Air Brigade in Comodoro Rivadavia (Chubut Province) where Operation Glaciar I was conducted. For the first time, the fighter-bombers carried out tactical navigations along the Argentinean Sea coast, reaching the Beagle Channel in Tierra del Fuego and the southern Andes Mountains. In September, the A-4s returned to this area of great geopolitical interest to carry out Glaciar II, operating from the Río Gallegos Military Air Base (Santa Cruz Province). As in Glaciar I, air-to-air and air-to-ground manoeuvres were carried out.

In August 2000, the Fightinghawks participated in the Operational Airspace Control Exercise Vigía III which had Resistencia Airport as its base of operations. On this occasion, the A-4ARs carried out aerial surveillance flights, interception of unidentified aircraft (without a flight plan) and reconnaissance of undeclared runways with the aim of cooperating in the fight against smuggling. For this type of manoeuvre, the ARG-1 radar demonstrated its full potential. These exercises continued over the following years, as it became more and more necessary to control the airspace of northern Argentina in the face of illegal flights, generally carrying drugs.

Exercise Cruzex 2004 in Brazil, the second version of the Cruzeiro do Sul exercise, took place between 3 and 20 November 2004 at the Natal Air Base and involved aircraft from the Air Forces of Argentina, Brazil, France and Venezuela. It was the largest exercise ever conducted in South America since the Second World War, involving more than 100 aircraft and helicopters of various types. For its part, the Argentine Air Force deployed six A-4AR Fightinghawk aircraft from the V Air Brigade, a Boeing 707, a C-130 and a KC-130 Hercules refuelling aircraft, all from the I Air Brigade.

Brazil, as host country, highlighted Embraer RA-1, A-1, A-1B and A-1A (AMX) aircraft from the 1st/16th Grupo de Aviaçao (GAv), 1st/10th GAv and 3rd/10th GAv, AT-26 Xavante from 1st/4th GAv, SC-95 and C-95 Bandeirante from different units, P-95 Bandeirulha from 1st/7th GAv, Mirage IIIBR from 1st Grupo de Defesa Aérea (1st GDA), Embraer Tucano from 1st/3rd GAv, Boeing KC-137 from 2nd/2nd/3rd GAv, F-5E Tiger II from 1st/14th GAv and 3rd/3rd GAv, Boeing KC-137 from 2nd/2nd/3rd GAv, F-5E Tiger II from 1st/14th GAv, Boeing KC-137 from 2nd/2nd/3rd GAv, F-5E Tiger II from 1st/14th GAv, 2nd/3rd GAv and 3rd/3rd GAv, F-5E Tiger II from 1st Grupo de Aviaçao de Caça and 1st/14th GAv, Boeing KC-137 from 2nd/2nd Transport Group (GT), Lockheed C-130H and KC-130H Hercules from 1st/1st GT, Embraer EMB-145SA (R-99A) early warning, EMB-145RS (R-99B) electronic warfare, both from 2nd/6th GAv and Learjet 35 from 1st/6th GAv. Helibras UH-50 Esquilo from the 2nd/8th GAv, UH-1H from the 1st/8th GAv and heavy CH-34 Super Puma from the 3rd/8th GAv were among the helicopters.

France was represented by a Boeing E-3F SDCA Sentry early warning aircraft, a Boeing KC-135 refueller from the 93rd Air Refuelling Group 'Bretagne', a Transall C-160 transport, a DC-8 and seven Mirage 2000RDI and 2000N (two-seat) fighters from the 2/12 'Picardie' squadron. The Venezuelan Air Force participated with six F-16A/B Grupo Aéreo de Caza 16, three Mirage 50EV/DV from Grupo Aéreo de Caza 11, Boeing 707-384C from Grupo Aéreo de Transporte 6 and AS-532 Cougar helicopters from Grupo Aéreo de Transporte 4.

This exercise was followed on 12–27 November 2005 by Ceibo 2005, held at the IV Air Brigade of the Argentine Air Force in Mendoza and the V Air Brigade, in which the air forces of Argentina, Brazil, Chile and Uruguay participated. The exercise was similar to Cruzex, with a coalition of aircraft from all countries fighting a fictitious enemy made up of A-4AR Fightinghawks and Mirage IIIEAs of the Argentine Air Force and also performing ground attack missions.

Argentina participated with one C-130B and one KC-130H, six IA-58A/D Pucará, two IA-63 Pampa, four FMA / Morane Saulnier MS-760 Paris, two SA-315B Lama, eight OA/A-4AR Fightinghawk, two Mirage 5A Mara, one Mirage IIIDA, six Mirage IIIEA, four IAI M5 Finger, two Bell 212 and one Fokker F-27. Brazil sent five AMX and one AMX-T, Uruguay three Cessna A-37B Dragonfly and Chile five Elkan single-seaters and one two-seater.

Subsequently, between 21 August and 1 September 2006, the third edition of the Cruzex took place at the Anápolis Air Base, in the state of Goiás, some 50 km from Brasilia, with a new participation of French Mirage 2000s, Argentina sending its A-4AR Fightinghawk and IA-58 Pucará, Uruguay with Pucará and Cessna A-37B, Venezuela with VF-5A, Mirage 50 and F-16, and Chile with A-37B. Although Peru was to participate with A-37s, a fatal accident during the deployment prevented them from being present. Brazil participated with A-1 AMX, A-29 Super Tucano, AT-26 Xavante, F-5E and F-5EM Tiger II, Bell UH-1H, H-34 Super Puma, H-50 Esquilo, Embraer R-99, SC-95 Bandeirante, T-27 Tucano, Boeing KC-137, KC-130/C-130 Hercules and Gates VU/R-35 LearJet.

This was the last time the A-4ARs participated in a Cruzex exercise, as they were unable to participate in the following editions in 2008, 2010 and 2013 due to political reasons.

However, between 25 and 30 October 2009, the A-4AR C-905, C-907, C-909, C-932 and C-935 and the OA-4AR C-902 participated together with a KC-130H Hercules and a Fokker F-28 of the FAA, in Exercise Salitre II at Cerro Moreno Air Base, Antofagasta, Chile, together with F-15C and D of the 122nd Fighter Squadron of the 149th Fighter Wing of the USAF, Mirage 2000C of the EC01.012 'Cambrésis' of the French Armée de l'Air, AMX of the 1st/10th GAv of the Força Aérea Brasileira and the F-5 of Aviation Group N°7, F-16A/B MLU of Aviation Group N°8 and F-16C/D of Aviation Group N°3 of the FACh, as well as support aircraft, a French E-3F Sentry, French KC-135FR, USAF KC-135R and Boeing 707 refuellers from Brazil and Chile.

Finally, from 6 to 17 October, they took part in Exercise Salitre III, where six A-4ARs were sent, along with four F-5EMs from the 1st/14th GAv, six F-16Cs from the 149th Fighter Wing of the Texas Air National Guard and three Cessna A-37Bs from Squadron 2 of Air Brigade II of the Uruguayan Air Force, in addition to the F-16A/B/C/Ds from Groups 3, 7 and 8 and F-5Es from Group 12 of the Chilean Air Force.

Operations and accidents

After more than seven years of intense operational service, the first serious accident occurred in 2005. At 13:30 on 6 July 2005, C-906 crashed to the ground in Paunero, near Chaján, in the province of Córdoba, 500m from the provincial border with San Luis and a few kilometres from its base in Villa Reynolds. The aircraft was manned by 29-year-old Lieutenant Horacio Martín Flores, who was killed in the late ejection. While performing combat manoeuvres, he entered a flat spin, from which only very experienced pilots can get out of. The pilot, perhaps feeling the pressure of fear of losing the first aircraft of this type, added to the short time he had been stationed at the base, having only just over 50 hours of flight time in this type of machine, did everything possible to save it, despite the repeated ejection order given to him by the section chief, who was flying alongside him, who replied 'I've got it', until it was too late to execute the ejection procedure and he started it the moment it hit the ground. On 24 August of the same year at 14:40, Fightinghawk registration C-936 also crashed to the ground 18km from Río Cuarto. The accident occurred during a check flight and the pilot managed to perform a controlled ejection, sustaining no injuries, while the machine was totally destroyed.

The last accident of the McDonnell Douglas A-4AR Fightinghawk of the Argentine Air Force was on 15 July 2024 and took the life of Captain Mauro Testa La Rosa, raising the question of the state of the veteran A-4AR fleet, which four years ago, on 5 August 2020, also cost the life of Captain Gonzalo Britos Venturini. Although there is still no preliminary report on the accident of the aircraft registered C-926, the testimonies of those who were able to see all the events indicate that it was a mechanical failure and that it would be related to the maintenance work that was carried out on the aircraft hours before attempting the take-off that ended in tragedy. As far as is known, according to some testimonies and as can be seen in a video of the accident, at the moment of reaching rotation speed to take off, the parachute container came off the plane and immediately smoke and then fire was seen coming out of the rear area of the fuselage, after which the pilot tried to gain altitude to eject. However, immediately after initiating ejection the aircraft exploded, preventing the parachute from opening.

Given the good relations with neighbouring countries, in addition to the constant budget cuts in which the Force was involved, as well as the cuts that were made in the A-4AR project itself, it was decided to preserve a certain number of aircraft, leaving in service the units necessary to complete pilot training and to demonstrate a minimum of deterrent power. The preservation techniques used for some aircraft were similar to the Naval Aviation Maintenance Programme, defined in the 'Preservation of Naval Aircraft' manual.

Due to the inefficiency of their 20mm Colt Mk 12 guns, the possibility of carrying out a modification similar to that executed with the veteran A-4B/Cs, installing the 30mm DEFA, was analysed, although it was determined that this could not be carried out, due to the lack of space because the on-board APU was located there, something that the old Skyhawk did not have.

The first real operation in which they took part was during the 4th Summit of the Americas, held in the city of Mar del Plata on 4 and 5 November 2005, in which, due to the participation of US President George W. Bush, an important protection operation had to be mounted, so the A-4ARs were deployed to the VI Air Brigade, in the city of Tandil, armed with Sidewinder missiles. There they operated under the control of two USAF E-3 Sentry aircraft, deployed to the Comandante Esporta Naval Air Base, in addition to a Westinghouse AN/TPS-43 FAA radar. This type of operation was repeated in August 2009, when the meeting of presidents of the Union of South American Nations (UNASUR) was held in the city of Bariloche.

Meanwhile, since 2007, they began to participate in Operation Fortin, a patrolling operation along the country's northern border, which was based on the experience acquired during the Vigía exercises. This operation was replaced in 2011 by Escudo Norte, which in turn was replaced in 2017 by Operativo Fronteras.

These tasks are also performed by FMA IA-63 Pampa and FMA IA-58A Pucará and since 2018 by Embraer Tucanos. The A-4s were initially deployed at Santiago del Estero airport, but currently operate from Resistencia, Chaco province, as well as Termas de Río Hondo, near Santiago del Estero.

Although aircraft attempt to intercept illegal flights, guided by ground-based radar, the lack of a law to shoot them down, to allow them to act if they intercept intruders, renders their operations ineffective, as they can only attempt to follow the intruder to its landing and give their position for security forces to act on, but usually the intruder aircraft return to their country of origin when intercepted, only to attempt the crossing again hours later.

In 2016, operational aircraft received the inscription 'Selecte 121.5' on the supplementary tanks, indicating the radio frequency to be selected by the intercepted aircraft.

The last accident occurred on 14 February 2013, when the C-902 crashed when it had engine problems while approaching the runway of the airport in the city of Santiago del Estero, as part of Operation Northern Shield to protect against illegal flights. The pilots, Major Machado and 1st Lieutenant Buossi ejected a few metres above the ground seconds before the aircraft hit the runway.

During the early years of the new millennium, the Dart 2 bombs were homologated on the Fightinghawk, which is a 227kg GPS and INS-guided bomb with wings that allow it to glide to reach a greater distance, reaching up to 60km. A small turbine-powered version (they use APUs from Mirage aircraft) allows it to reach over 200km, making it virtually a cruise missile.

Because the aircraft were initially planned to be in service for only ten years, since 1997, they are currently suffering from a lack of spare parts and adequate logistical support, leading to a significant part of the fleet being grounded and, at the end of 2017, only two single-seaters and one two-seater being in service.

A growing problem is the difficulties in obtaining spare parts, as Boeing (after buying McDonnell Douglas) is no longer supporting the model and, with fewer and fewer operators, availability is decreasing.

They are currently equipped with AIM-9M Sidewinder air-to-air missiles, 125kg and 250kg Expal and similar general-purpose bombs produced in Argentina, 500kg Mk 17, the so-called 'Bombolas' (old 454kg AN M65 bombs, with a Mk 17 tail), LAU-61 rockets with nineteen 70mm tubes and LAU-10 with four 127mm tubes, and the FAS 850 Dardo 1 and Dardo 2 standoff bombs have been evaluated, among other locally produced weapons. Mk 106 2.3kg and Mk 76 12kg exercise bombs are used for bombing practice.

The A-4ARs now carry the full weight of the Argentine Air Force's air defence and strike missions, since the Mirages were retired in November 2015.

One of their main missions is to patrol the country's northern border, due to the increasing activity of illegal flights from Bolivia and Paraguay, generally carrying contraband and drugs. For this purpose, Operation Fortin began in 2007, replaced since 2011 by Operation Northern Shield.

These tasks are also performed by FMA IA-63 Pampa and FMA IA-58A Pucará, while until 2014 they were also performed by Mirages. The A-4s were initially deployed to Santiago del Estero airport, while the Mirages were deployed to Resistencia or the city of Posadas. Currently, A-4ARs operate at both Resistencia and Termas de Río Hondo, close to Santiago del Estero. The Pucarás operate from their base at the III Air Brigade in Reconquista or deploy to other cities, as in the case of Posadas. The Pampa has generally operated from Santiago del Estero. Embraer Emb-312 Tucano aircraft from the Military Aviation School are currently being considered for such missions.

In 2016, operational aircraft received the inscription 'Selecte 121.5' on the supplementary tanks, indicating the radio frequency to be selected by intercepted aircraft.

Last mission

When Argentina was selected to chair the G20, which brings together the world's twenty largest economies, the problem of providing the necessary security for the leaders' summit, due to take place on 30 November and 1 December 2018, soon emerged. The main concern was the lack of an adequate fighter force to provide air protection, with only three Fightinghawks operational by the end of 2017. While it was decided to go ahead with the Navy's plans to buy five Super Étendards to restore its air strike and air defence capability, a delay in the process prevented them from getting there in time. Moreover, while the budget to buy twelve new fighters for up to $600 million to replace the A-4s was approved for 2017 and also for 2018, the government ultimately decided to delay those plans.

Without the decision to purchase new aircraft, the MoD realized that they would have to rely on what was already available and work got underway to have as many A-4s, Pucarás and Pampas in operation to provide air cover. In October 2018, Fightinghawks deployed to Resistencia to control illegal flights, but also conducted night air-to-air refuelling for the first time, from a KC-130H Hercules. This capability had been abandoned in 1985 and had never been used with A-4ARs.

After that, between 15 and 23 November they deployed to the VI Air Brigade in Tandil, along with Pampas, Pucarás, Hercules and Bell 212 and 412s for Exercise Integrator 2018. The main activities of the A-4s were air-to-air combat with Sidewinder and gunships, including combat against Pucarás and Pampas. According to Major Carlos Glahs, both aircraft are very difficult to catch in close air combat, as their turn radius is very tight and they can fly very slowly. 'With radar you can easily catch it (the Pucará), it (the Pampas) is very big. The problem is to avoid a dogfight, because you can't close the Pucará's turn. You have to shoot and run,' explains Glahs.

In addition, for the first time, the A-4ARs conducted air-to-air gunfire against a target towed by a Pucará, and night refuelling and air-to-ground operations were conducted.

Following the exercise, five A-4ARs deployed to the I Air Brigade, in the suburbs of Buenos Aires, along with five Pucarás and four Pampas to meet the challenge of providing air cover over the city on the two days of the summit. The USAF deployed two Sentrys to assist in early warning, operating alongside the Air Force's five ground-based radars.

The Fightinghawks flew 30 hours in pairs during those two days, and the rest of the time the Pampas and Pucarás took over the mission. In the end, they did not need to be refuelled in the air during the sorties, which lasted an average of two hours, but the two KC-130Hs were ready to refuel them if necessary. They always flew armed with two AIM-9M Sidewinders and the guns. Fortunately, there were no interceptions as no intruders were detected.

Protecting the world's most important leaders was the most important mission for the former Fightinghawk and, despite fears that they could not provide air cover for the entire summit, they accomplished the mission.

Future

Given the critical state of the fleet, with few operational aircraft and a lack of spare parts, work is underway to select a replacement, with a decision expected in 2025. The two models under consideration are the Leonardo M-346FA and the KAI FA-50, with some favouritism towards the Korean model, given its better combat performance. The plan for now is to buy ten to twelve units. Thus, it is estimated that the A-4AR will leave active service around 2027 ending the era of the A-4 Skyhawk in Argentina.

The US Marine Corps A-4M Bureau Number 159778, later to become C-914 in the Argentine Air Force.

C-905, still as an A-4M and with the initial paint scheme that the first two aircraft used in the United States. (*Photo Lockheed Skunk Works*)

The C-906 'Gaucho 01' during the first flights in the United States. This airframe would later be replaced due to structural problems. (*Photo Lockheed Skunk Works*)

An A-4AR undergoes radar emission testing in the United States during pre-delivery programme evaluation. (*Photo Lockheed Skunk Works*)

A-4M cells are brought to A-4AR standard at LMAASA hangar 90 in Cordoba, Argentina. (*Photo LMAASA*)

The A-4AR registration C-906 performing Mk 82 bomb drop tests with Snakeye braked tail in the United States. (*Photo Lockheed Skunk Works*)

An OA-4AR and three A-4ARs from the first batch delivered making a formation flight in the United States. (*Photo Lockheed Skunk Works*)

One of the OA-4ARs just out of the workshop where it was modernized in the United States, after a test flight. (*Photo Lockheed Skunk Works*)

Due to bad weather in Tegucigalpa, one of their stops on the flight to Argentina, aircraft on the second ferry make an unscheduled stop at Guatemala City's La Aurora airport in May 1998.

Five A-4ARs fly over Mount Fitzroy or Chaltén, on the border between Argentina and Chile, at the southern tip of Patagonia. (*Photo Daniel Berástegui*)

Antenna of the A-4AR's ARG-1 radar. Basically an APG-66 with a smaller antenna. (*Photo Horacio Clariá*)

An A-4AR refuelling an A-4B using the Buddy Pack system. The A-4Bs and Cs coexisted for less than two years with the A-4ARs.

An A-4AR with eight 130kg IMI PG 130 Mk 3 bombs shortly after its arrival in the country.

An A-4AR with an AN M-65 'Bombola' bomb on its belly mount. These bombs were originally used in Argentina on the Avro Lancaster and Lincoln.

In March 1998 the A-4AR C-930 participated together with an IA-63 Pampa in the FIDAE show in Santiago de Chile. It was the only time an A-4 took part in the fair. (*Photo Patrick Laureau*)

Emblem of the A-4AR programme.

Emblem of Fighter Group 5.

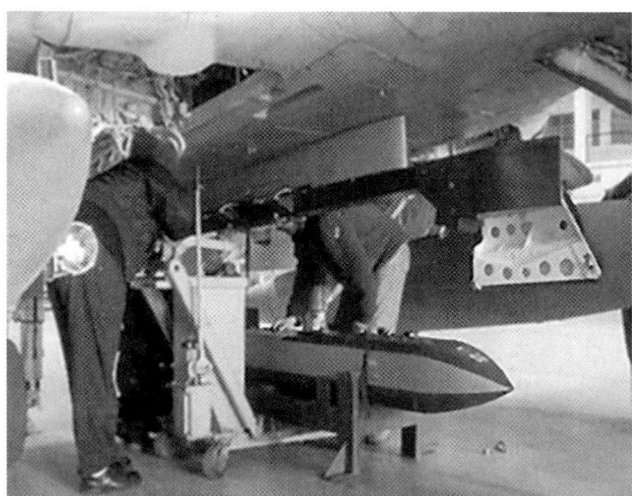

A Dart 2 bomb is loaded into an A-4AR during trials for type approval. Currently, although not operationally adopted, it is the most modern air-to-surface weaponry fitted to the Fightinghawk.

Flight line during Exercise Icarus at III Air Brigade in 2010, with four A-4ARs alongside an IAI M5 Finger, a two-seat M5 Dagger, a Mirage IIIDA, a Mirage IIIEA and two IA-63 Pampas.

An OA-4AR armed with AN M65 454kg bombs on the sub-wing supports and a supplementary tank on the ventral support.

Captain Claudio Loveira inspects the Mk 12 practice bombs on the A-4AR C-934 before leaving on a training flight in March 2001. (*Photo Santiago Rivas*)

An A-4AR in flight armed with 250kg Expal BR bombs on the belly mount.

AIM-9M missile with warhead on an A-4AR during the Summit of the Americas in November 2005. To provide security on those days, the aircraft operated in conjunction with USAF Boeing E-3 Sentry early warning aircraft deployed to the Comandante Espora Naval Air Station.

An A-4AR equipped with Mk 12 practice bombs rolls towards the head of the V Air Brigade runway in March 2001. (*Photo Santiago Rivas*)

Fifteen Fightinghawks, both single-seat and two-seat, alongside the C-130H Hercules, registration TC-68, at V Air Brigade on 14 March 1999.

An OA-4AR equipped with an ACMI Ehud pod takes off in 2000 from the V Air Brigade. (*Photo Santiago Rivas*)

An A-4AR alongside an Alabama National Guard F-16C and an FAA Bell 212 at V Air Brigade during Exercise Eagle 1 in 1998. (*Photo Santiago Rivas*)

An A-4AR and a Mirage IIIEA escort an F-16C of the District of Columbia National Guard over the 5th Air Brigade during Exercise Eagle II.

An A-4AR in flight, carrying an AIM-9M exercise missile.

Refuelling an A-4AR using the pro≠≠be. (*Photo Guillermo Galmarini*)

An A-4AR in flight near its base in 2000. (*Photo Hernán Casciani*)

A Fightinghawk operating in the rain at its base. (*Photo Santiago Rivas*)

Two A-4ARs flying over Mendoza province in November 2005, during the Ceibo exercise. (*Photo Fabio Núñez*)

Bottom view of an A-4AR with everything down. (*Photo Santiago Rivas*)

The C-909 at Anápolis Air Base, Brazil, during the Cruzex III exercise in 2006.

During the second edition of the Salitre exercise in Chile in 2009, A-4ARs flew alongside USAF F-15Cs, French Mirage 2000Cs, Brazilian AMXs and Chilean Air Force F-16A MLUs, as seen in the picture.

US National Guard F-16Cs alongside an A-4AR during Exercise Salitre III in 2014. (*Photo Germán Bossio*)

An A-4AR refuelling in flight from a KC-130 in 2009. (*Photo Santiago Rivas*)

During the Precruzex exercise in 2008, A-4ARs were prepared at the III Air Brigade to participate in the Cruzex exercise in Brazil. Unfortunately, the nation's congress did not arrive in time to authorize the departure of the Argentine contingent, which was unable to participate in the multinational exercise. (*Photo Santiago Rivas*)

An A-4AR makes a low-altitude pass in front of the V Air Brigade control tower in September 2010. (*Photo Santiago Rivas*)

An A-4AR takes off from its base with an AIM-9M Sidewinder exercise missile. The aircraft carries the emblem of the Salitre II exercise. (*Photo Santiago Rivas*)

A Fightinghawk during night training in 2011. (*Photo Santiago Rivas*)

An A-4AR using its parachute on landing at its base. (*Photo Santiago Rivas*)

An A-4AR landing at III Airborne Brigade in 2010, armed with an exercise Sidewinder. (*Photo Santiago Rivas*)

Take-off and turnaround of an A-4AR at the V Air Brigade in 2011. (*Photo Santiago Rivas*)

Cockpit of the A-4AR, where the two multifunction screens and the HUD in the centre can be seen.

An OA-4AR and an A-4AR are silhouetted against the sun during a pass over the IX Air Brigade at Comodoro Rivadavia on 1 May 2011, during the anniversary of the FAA's baptism of fire in the Malvinas. (*Photo Santiago Rivas*)

Take-off of the C-905 of the III Air Brigade, with the pilot picking up the landing gear immediately after getting the wheels off the ground.

Index